# A WOR
# DIFFE

## THE BIG GREEN POETRY MACHINE

Recycle, Recycle, Recycle! Love the world you live in. Be good to your planet. Don't be mean, be green! Recycle, Recycle, Recycle! Love the world you live in. Be good to your planet. Don't be mean, be green! Recycle, Recycle, Recycle! Love the world you live in. Be good to your planet. Don't be mean, be green! Recycle, Recycle, Recycle! Love the world

# Verses From The Midlands

### Edited by Vivien Linton

First published in Great Britain in 2009 by:

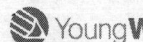 Young**Writers**

Young Writers
Remus House
Coltsfoot Drive
Peterborough
PE2 9JX
Telephone: 01733 890066
Website: www.youngwriters.co.uk

# Foreword

Young Writers' A World of Difference is a showcase for our nation's most brilliant young poets to share their thoughts, hopes and fears for the planet they call home.

Young Writers was established in 1990 to nurture creativity in our children and young adults, to give them an interest in poetry and an outlet to express themselves. Seeing their work in print will encourage them to keep writing as they grow, and become our poets of tomorrow.

Selecting the poems has been challenging and immensely rewarding. The effort and imagination invested by these young writers makes their poems a pleasure to enjoy reading time and time again.

# Contents

# The Poems

# Human Waste

Recycling, recycling,
How can it be?
Just pick up the rubbish
And you'll be happy.

Rubbish, rubbish,
How dirty it can be,
So clean it up
And now it's history.

Recycling, recycling,
How can it be?
Just pick up the rubbish
And now it's history!

Rubbish, rubbish,
How dirty it can be,
So clean it up
And you'll be happy!

**Hannah Clapinson (12)**
Casterton Business & Enterprise College, Stamford

# Untitled

Melting, melting
The ice caps are melting
Stop driving big cars
Start with small
Tides are rising
No folk diving
As seas are rising.

**James McGeorge (12)**
Casterton Business & Enterprise College, Stamford

# Don't Die World

The grass is green,
The sky is blue,
Why can't I see this?
Why can't you?

The sky is black,
The grass is brown,
What has happened to the world?
I feel so down.

Anger and hate is all around
It's in the air, it's in the ground
Animals hurt, trees cut down.

Alone in the world,
Fall to the ground.
No one to love,
No one to hug,
Die alone.
Don't live for long.
The world is dead,
Your love is gone.
Pollution, death,
Can't go on,
It must be stopped
We need help . . . anyone?

**Chloe Glover (12)**
Casterton Business & Enterprise College, Stamford

# Recycle

Recycle, then you can get a motorcycle
If you don't turn the light off at night they won't always be as bright!
If you are nice to God instead of being a little sod
You will get a lot more out of life!

**Daniel Parker (12)**
Casterton Business & Enterprise College, Stamford

# Think About The Animals

Think about the animals
For they are in cages overfilled.
The elephants are dying every day
Do we really want life to be this way?
Lions, giraffes and monkeys are being kept away
From their natural habitat where they should stray.
Think about the baby animals out there alone,
Their mothers have been shot so the baby has no home.
Animals have rights of their own
So let them live in the wild alone
With no poachers to ruin their homes.
So next time you're looking for animal coats
Think about the animals!

**Alex Meagre (12)**
Casterton Business & Enterprise College, Stamford

# Matters On Earth

Greenhouse gases, what does it mean?
Letting things get to a certain extreme.
Children, animals, adults too
Nature's beauty, it's up to you.
Why do we ruin such a wonderful thing?
We all wanna live in a world free of sin.
Why are animals and children abused?
They're all part of our worldly views.

**Jemma Schulze (12)**
Casterton Business & Enterprise College, Stamford

# War

Bullets whizzing over my head, an explosion nearby .
Crouching in the darkness, death, shadows creeping by.
Innocent men being snatched away from light, dragged into nothing.
People sat at home waiting for them,
Not realising that they're never going to see them again.

**Kerouac Andrews (12)**
Casterton Business & Enterprise College, Stamford

# Naughty And Bad

I'm in my room hiding from my dad
He calls me naughty, he calls me bad.
He comes into my room at night
And hits me when Mum's out of sight.
Mummy thinks it's bullies at school
Cos of my bruises and all
I long to tell her it's my dad
But he will call me naughty, he will call me bad.

**Beth Downing (12)**
Casterton Business & Enterprise College, Stamford

# Litter

Litter, litter everywhere,
Litter, litter does anyone care?
Litter, litter full of disease,
Litter, litter gives a bad breeze.
Litter, litter smells of fish
Litter, litter not on my dish.
Litter, litter, doom around the bend
Litter, litter should come to an end!

**Joshua Carter-Begbie (13)**
Casterton Business & Enterprise College, Stamford

# The Recycle Poem

Change the world and recycle
Collecting cans, paper, bottles, every little helps
Pack your kit and do your bit
Use bags for life.
Walk, don't drive,
Feel more alive.
Please recycle.

**William Pearce (12)**
Casterton Business & Enterprise College, Stamford

# The Rainforest Going

The rainforest so green it glows, the wooden trunks so tall
The soil so moist, the ground so wet.
They help us breathe by making oxygen
They look so good, high in the sky
Towering over all who wander through.
The next you know there's a *bang!*
Trucks going to and from the forest
Chainsaws cutting them down
The next you know, they're gone forever.

**Jack Hollingworth (12)**
Casterton Business & Enterprise College, Stamford

# We Can Change The World

Ice caps are melting
Animals are dying
The rainforests are on the brink
And the children are crying.

Humans aren't caring
But there's something we can do
Stop pollution and global warming
And make our sky more blue.

**Connor Breakell (12)**
Casterton Business & Enterprise College, Stamford

# Trapped

I am the chains that restrain me
I am the ropes that hang me
I am the fire that burns me
Forever I am trapped.

I am the water that drowns me
Nobody cares though
I am forever trapped
In the fire that burns me
And the ropes that hang me.

Nobody has done anything wrong
Why am I trapped anyway?
One day I will know
Mother said there is peace out there
I doubt it . . .

**Daniel Burwood (12)**
Casterton Business & Enterprise College, Stamford

# Killing Off The Animals

So many animals have already been lost
Others are on the way out at a great cost
Because we are chopping down the forests,
Animals have nowhere to go or live.
Poachers fly over in their choppers
Then they even get lucky and evade the coppers.
Leaving rubbish behind doesn't help
Birds and other animals getting caught
Dodos are gone so are the dinos
On the way are the tigers and rhinos.
So if we don't stop, think and help,
We will lose lots of the world's beautiful nature.

**Lawrence Copeman (12)**
Casterton Business & Enterprise College, Stamford

# War

Make it stop, stop, stop
Or they'll drop, drop, drop
With a medal in their sight
Whilst fighting with all of their might.

It could be our friend or family
As they hold their gun firmly
If they stand up ready
Or lie down steady.

People will always be killed
As you see we are not thrilled
As the country is alerted
And places are deserted
And the battle will go on and on and on.

**Natasha Smith (12)**
Casterton Business & Enterprise College, Stamford

# The Litter Bin

I'm the litter bin and I am very upset
People don't put their rubbish in me
They throw it down or walk past
And my bin bags always last,
They are always empty.

One day I'm full and one day I am not
But I only get emptied every two months
So I am overflowing with rubbish lumps,
With rats at my feet, I'm smelly and dirty.

You need to help me out so we don't get anymore litter about
We have to stop global warming and keep our planet clean.

**Charlie Press (12)**
Casterton Business & Enterprise College, Stamford

# The Litter Muncher

I'm disgusted,
Rubbish all over
Rats, mice, all sorts
Why don't we shove it over the White Cliffs of Dover?
So put a stop to this while we can
Stranded animals munching away
And all we have is storms all May
So put a stop to this while we can
Think of all the creatures you're nurturing
Stop this and stop skirting
This is going beyond all sins
So put your rubbish in the bins
Put a stop to this while we can.

**Tim Taylor (13)**
Casterton Business & Enterprise College, Stamford

# Global Warming

The ice is melting,
The air is warming,
The sea is rising,
The people are starving.
Polar bears are approaching their death
Their habitats will slowly disappear
It's all going slowly, so stand and assist.
Hurricanes start to approach,
It blew a car into a coach.
Heat begins to rise
So we need to rise and help ourselves survive.

**Victoria Rose (12)**
Casterton Business & Enterprise College, Stamford

# Why Should I Bother?

Why should I bother to care for the Earth
For when I'm dead, what's it worth?
Litter is dropped everywhere
But it's all picked up so why should I care?
Global warming is on its last lap
And the Earth is too, but it's dead last
When global warming reaches the end
Then that is it, we cannot pretend
That the Earth is fine, the Earth is clear
And now global warming is ever nearer.
'It *should* worry you, it *should* scare you'
Is what they all say
But why me? It's not gonna happen today!

**Ellie James (12)**
Casterton Business & Enterprise College, Stamford

# Untitled

It does not matter if you're black or white, foreign or English
You will always be part of the world.
You would not like it if someone was picking on you day and night
Making fights because of your skin colour.

**Tonisha Bloodworth (12)**
Casterton Business & Enterprise College, Stamford

# Animals' Rights!

Death, death all around
As innocent animals fall to the ground.
Whilst hundreds of species are wiped out
Ivory tusks sell for big amounts.
All around us day by day
Animals lose the right to play.
We shoot and kill the animal folk
We're all responsible, that's no joke!

**Katrina Miles (12)**
Casterton Business & Enterprise College, Stamford

# Kids Job To Clean Up The Mess!

I woke up one morning and went into my street
Disgustingly I went out to meet . . .
A pile of rubbish as big as a house,
I think I even saw a mouse!

I don't know why, I don't know how
But what I do know is what is happening now!
Countries are sinking and people are dying
Mostly because those planes keep flying.

The worst thing is that we're doing wrong
We're destroying where other people belong.
So as this world is being lost
We need to defend it at all cost.

Though we are only growing up slow
It is time for the parents to go.
We're starting to like them even less
It's up to us kids to clean up *their* mess!

**Josh Topley (13)**
Casterton Business & Enterprise College, Stamford

# The Homeless

I'm cold, I want food, I'm alone, I have no home.
It happened when my house got burnt to ash.
My life began to change, so now I live on the streets of London.
I'm dying, people hate me, even my best friend hates me!
I've never washed, every night I pray and every day.
All I want is a house;
To anyone out there please help homeless people get a home.

**George Brecknock (12)**
Casterton Business & Enterprise College, Stamford


# Global Threat

The world is heating up like a microwave
The ice is melting to make a lemonade.
Animals are going, the Earth is not showing
It's a struggle to breathe and is shutting down.
The world is dying and we are frying
This beautiful place is dying at an alarming pace.

**Jodie Hunt (12)**
Casterton Business & Enterprise College, Stamford

# Being Green

Being green
What does it really mean?
Being literally a tree
Or painting yourself green?

It's saving the world - that's all the talk
Talking about the pollution - that worries us
And this evident desolation
It truly scares us, it really does.

Then I have to think a little longer
What does it all really mean?
One tiny piece of litter
Or those machines going clank and scream?

It's all this so-called greenhouse gas
And the expert's advice we hear at night.
'Turn off that TV at the mains
And all those unused lights when it's bright.'

They all create such a fuss
I really want to help, honest I do.
It's all just so annoying
What a difference will I make too?

Maybe if we all did pitch in
Instead of leaving it for everyone else.
Take matters into our own hands
And the problems just might be dealt with.

So if we all helped by recycling something
Just one small piece to make sure we do our bit
The rubbish could be recycled into something cool
Instead of being chucked into a bottomless pit.

So please, please join me
On my quest to save our precious Earth
We would be known as superheroes
And who knows how much our efforts could be worth.

So keep up the good work
So in the future people will see
The beautiful baby polar bears
And an unburnt tree!

**Kirsty Maguire (12)**
Cheadle High School, Cheadle

# Green To Keep It

The world is big
The world is mean
We need to keep it green.

If that means growing your own food
Or recycling your waste
Do what you can to help the mood
Of the world in haste.

Pick up the litter that seems to filter
Between the scenes that seem to glitter
It's the rubbish that spoils it
That's why you need to do your bit
So please, just think about the world apart
Which will touch you right at heart.

**Natasha Christy (13)**
Cordeaux School, Louth

# Hope

Dear Mammoth
We are making you extinct. We're dreadfully sorry but your luxurious fur is very valuable

Yours truly
P Ollution.

Dear P Bear
We're very sorry but your iceberg home is an eyesore. We are replacing it with a Jacuzzi. Your new home is next to the local chippie.

Yours truly
G Warming

Dear Sirs, Mammoth and P Bear,
We are helping you and the rest of the world. Your home and fur are being recovered.There is hope!

Yours sincerely
Bluepeace.

**Matt Anderson (11)**
Dagfa House School, Nottingham

# Tank

The tank is a deadly thing, it's already killed 1,000 trees.
It hasn't fired a single round, all it's done is crawl across the ground.
Shermans, Pancers and A7Xs, they're nasty to humans but lethal to trees.
The main ammunition doesn't come out of the gun,
It comes out the exhaust with the engine's hum.
If the tank continues to pollute and cause death the birds will not sing for no trees shall be left.

**Jacob Oleshko (11)**
Dagfa House School, Nottingham

# World Problems

Up with brown bins, down with black bins
The ozone layer is disappearing.
Greenhouse gases spreading all over
What can we do to help?

Mustard gas and cluster bombs, terrorists and nukes
It doesn't matter what colour you are
Why can't we all be friends?

Trees and plants turned into paper
Rainforest turned into fields
So what will we do when the oxygen's gone?

*Splish, splash*
What's that I hear?
It's acid rain on my windowpane.

So hear me now
Where's Mr Mammal?
Oh yeah, he's dead.
His tusks are hanging above my bed,
His fur as a blanket keeps me warm.

So don't ever litter
Don't ever spit
So let's great rid of the carbon footprint.

**Aria Shahrokhshahi (12)**
Dagfa House School, Nottingham

# Racism

Just too much racism, people think it's funny
But it really hurts the person if they're a Jew or a Sikh.
The world would be a better place if there were no racism.
You're black, you're white, I just don't know why they do it.
It is stupid, it is not funny, there's just way too much racism.
Wouldn't the world be a better place if there were no racism?

**Joshua Kingsley (13)**
Dagfa House School, Nottingham

# Wars

World War I
Left lots dead.
You want a break,
Here's World War II instead.
World War II,
More are killed
Then with war,
Korea killed.
Vietnam,
More are dead.
Then the Gulf
But why no war?
Why not peace instead?

**Edward Orme-Claye (11)**
Dagfa House School, Nottingham

# Litter

Mess mess all around
Being thrown to the ground
Tin cans, sweet wrappers, plastic bottles
Why do we do it?

Burger wrappers, spitting gum
Remains of packed lunches we got from Mum.
Banana skins and apple cores
Why do we do it?

Put it in the bottle bank
Put it in the bin
Recycle it to make new things
Save our world.

**Laura Seymour (12)**
Dagfa House School, Nottingham

# Save The Rainforest

You are the killers of the Earth
And you deserve to die
I love trees and will forever
If it's a job then find another
Because trees save us for all time
They take in carbon dioxide and feed us air
So why kill them?
When you can get a save the rainforest bear.

Our little four-legged creatures
Don't benefit from this either
They soon will die through lack of food
And we will be to blame for what has happened
Because we killed the trees
And did that for crops like peas.
Save the rainforest
OK, please!

**Thomas Hopcroft (12)**
Dagfa House School, Nottingham

# There Once Was A Man

There once was a man with scars on his face
He was treated this way because of his race.
They did this to him because of prejudice or fright
The man was black and the bullies were white.
The fight was wrong
Though the man stood strong
As a crowd looked on
He was beaten and his blood ran red
The gang and crowd still left him for dead.
There once was a man with scars on his face
He was treated this way because of his race.

**Christian McLeod (11)**
Dagfa House School, Nottingham

# Pollution Is Poison

Cars
Trucks
Lorries
Taxis
Pollution
Trains
Cruisers
Tanks
Motorbikes
Pollution
Factories
Power plants
Oil rigs
Us
Pollution.

Even though we blame these things, *we* are the real criminals
We drive, we pollute, we work, we pollute, we cannot stop polluting.
But there's hope, recycling, biking, walking
These are the antidotes to the poison we have created.

**Matthew Peddle (11)**
Dagfa House School, Nottingham

# Endangered Species

Animals dead for their skin
Animals dead for their tusks
People killing just for fun
People killing for their meat
Plants, their homes disappearing
Plants, their food getting chopped down
Extinction happening because of pollution
Extinction happening because of people!

**Ainsley Lau (11)**
Dagfa House School, Nottingham

# Will It Be . . .

In 1,000 years what will this world be?
Will it be covered in rubbish?
Will there even be enough of it left to see
Or will it just evaporate in one almighty swish?

Will it be full of floating flats
Or will we all own our own jets?
Will it be ruled by alien cats
Or will we all owe massive debts?

Will it be a glamorous place
Or will it be a land of fear?
Will it be overruled by a powerful race
Or will it be a place of tears?

Will it be a great big dump
Or will it be a technical age?
Will it be less than a stump
Or will it be inside a massive cage?

Whatever the world is in 1,000 years
Whether it's full of tears or fears
It's up to you how it turns out!

**Edward Andrew Gray (12)**
Dagfa House School, Nottingham

# Empty World

People are starving they need food and drink
They don't have a family but we do
So we need to raise money to give to them
The children don't have an education because they have to work
We are lucky we don't get diseases
We can give things to charity, they will send the things to the poor people in
the world
People will get better things than what they have got now
Let's get to work and help the poor people in the world.

**Paige Tien (12)**
Dagfa House School, Nottingham


# Litter

Children throw litter away because they think they are cool.
There is a bin so the dustbin men come and collect it, so why do they throw it
on the floor?
They are silly people and it pollutes the world and it will be a dirty world
So just think what you do to the world next time when you litter
Just pick it up and put it in the bin and it will make you feel good
And our world will be a better place.

**James Crawford (11)**
Dagfa House School, Nottingham


# Don't Start

Don't start to litter or else you'll be bitter.
Don't start a war; you'll end on the floor.
Don't start to kill, stick to our will
Save us today, it will go a long way
Stick to it.

**Joe Bendeer (12)**
Dagfa House School, Nottingham

# Pollution

People make more factories, this world will go bust
Leaving the world in a blanket of dust
But it's not just factories, we must do something, we must, *must!*
The pollution will also start to affect animals and in some animals, their tusks
So we must start acting soon or if we don't
You've seen what could happen
So if you are reading this, please act *now!*

**Rohit Assi (11)**
Dagfa House School, Nottingham

# War

Flowers being trampled, shots being fired,
People dropping like flies,
This is war.
War brings tears to our eyes,
Death to our families.
This isn't us,
We're humans,
Proud and cheerful, love spreads through our race,
Families and friends.
But war, war pulls us apart,
All of us,
War makes us killers.

War,
War,
War makes us killers.
War destroys,
War destroys,
War destroys our souls

**Samuel Dare (11)**
Dagfa House School, Nottingham

# Pollution

The world is dying, day by day
And people are homeless, day by day.
Trees are dying, day by day,
Animals are dying, day by day.
Paper is dying, day by day
Plants are dying, day by day.

We can help
By walking to school,
Riding to school,
By recycling.

**Alasdair Tilson (11)**
Dagfa House School, Nottingham

# Animals Becoming Extinct

Animals are becoming extinct
Being killed for their fur
Being killed for meat

Chopping down trees, no place for birds
Throwing litter onto the floor, strangling animals in plastic bags
Look around when driving, don't do road kill!

Save our fluffy friends
Don't be a murderer!

**Katie Shipman (12)**
Dagfa House School, Nottingham

# Homeless People

The world is getting worse
People are being kicked out of their homes
Homeless people should be able to have a home
People are out at night, really hungry and cold
Sleeping on a bench with no gold.

**Daniel Bartlam (11)**
Dagfa House School, Nottingham

# Our Planet

This is our planet and we should treat it with respect
And an example of life and people dying with our regret.
Rainforests and recycling are just two of the things we forget.
Poverty all over the world with people with no water or food to eat
With pollution ruling our streets
And as we wonder what we should do
It'll be too late and our planet will be gone.
But if we all work together as a team we will stop the global terrors from ruling
the world.

**Simran Aujla (11)**
Dagfa House School, Nottingham

# You're Killing The Rainforest

*You're killing the rainforest*
Veins are snapping
Animals aren't chatting
Trees are falling
Everybody's crawling.

*You're killing the rainforest*
No more canopies
Where are the trees?
Seeds aren't growing
No trees showing.

*You're killing the rainforest*
Dangers ahead
The rainforest will soon be dead
Stop before it's too late

*You're killing the rainforest!*

**Abby Nield (12)**
Dagfa House School, Nottingham

# A Green Summer

I want a summer that's green,
I want a summer with plants,
I want a summer with trees,
I want a summer with happiness and a summer with bees.
If people stop and don't be green
Then there will not be a summer of green.

I want a summer of love,
I want a summer with happiness,
I want a summer with fun,
I want a summer that's green.

**Leon Ratcliff (11)**
Dagfa House School, Nottingham

# The Old Stately Home

I walk down a corridor in an old stately home
Separated from tourists, I walk alone.
I walk through a door and into a room
With a gilded carpet and a painted ceiling
High arched windows and a forgotten feeling
But I'm surrounded by objects big and small
A zoo of stuffed animals in an old stately hall.
A grizzly bear with wide brown paws
Decaying fur and no claws.
A crocodile with jaws open wide
Missing the teeth on either side.
Perched up high, a family of falcons
All losing feathers without any talons.
A once proud lion with a golden hide
But a scraggly mane without its pride.
An animal kingdom all denied their freedom
Lost and forgotten in an old stately home.

**Harriet Cheshire (12)**
Dagfa House School, Nottingham

# Pollution

The world is getting hotter
The world is filled with smog
This is caused by factories
This is caused by cars
The car releases carbon
The cow releases methane
The carbon fills the air
The carbon makes you cough.
The plants absorb the gases
The plants exhale oxygen.

**Robert Flatley (11)**
Dagfa House School, Nottingham

# War - Why Do We Have It?

War - why do we have it?
To stop fighting?
I think not.
Many mothers have lost their brave sons and daughters
To people they'll never know.
Our fighting tears the world apart,
Turns Muslims to terrorists like 9/11.
Let Iraq sort out its own problems
Afghanistan has got its own government.
War is good for absolutely nothing.

**Daniel Green (11)**
Dagfa House School, Nottingham

# Wake Up

Iraq, it fills the air with noises
When a bullet hits the ground.
Is someone going to die in vain today
All in the name of the government?

Civilians struck with terror
Soldiers killed by friendly fire
Who is next
You?
All in the name of the government.

Don't fight for the majority stand up for the minority
Stand up for what is right - even if you stand alone
Wake up.

**Damon Coyle (11)**
Dagfa House School, Nottingham

# Where Did All The Green Go?

Green was the colour of the grass
Green was the colour of the leaves
Green was the colour of the leaves on the trees
Green was the colour of life

Few seconds later . . .

There was no grass
There were no flowers
There were no trees
There was no green
Where did all the green go?

**Amandeep Kalirai (13)**
Dagfa House School, Nottingham

# Saving The World

People come together
To help save the world
They are worried
To see what's happening.
Too much traffic
Is killing the world.
All the pollution
It's not helping.
Using a bike
Is a good idea.
Why not walk
Instead of driving.
Look around at our wonderful world.

**Fraser Strafford-Taylor (13)**
Dagfa House School, Nottingham

# Save The Planet

The planet is ours and ours it is
For we know what to do
But what we do is this
We destroy, we dismay
We discharge and display.

The planet is ours and ours it is
For we know what to do
And now what we do is this
Make happiness, make more
Make peace and no war.

**Kelly Johnston (12)**
Dagfa House School, Nottingham

# Earth . . . Litter . . . Pollution . . . Trees . . .

Earth, we are killing the Earth
What can we do?
We can stop killing it and start saving it.
Give it the medicine, the Earth needs it.

Litter, when we have a drink what do we do with the can?
Chuck it on the floor
What are we supposed to do?
Put it in the bin because it's our job.

Pollution, bikes are gone, horses are gone
What do we use?
Cars, cars and more cars
They let off pollution, a gas that hurts the Earth!

Trees, what do we do to trees?
Chop them down!
Do they give us anything?
Yes, oxygen, so why do we kill them?

Earth, we are killing the Earth
What can we do?
We can stop killing it and start saving it.
Give it the medicine, the Earth needs it.

**Connor Donson (12)**
Dagfa House School, Nottingham

# The Lion's Mane

The golden fur such a lush mane
All replaced with mange
Juicy prey so delicious and sweet
Replaced with maggots, not a treat
Broad muscles ready for the hunt
Weak and useless, moving makes him grunt
The loudest roar causing fear
Just a growl causes a tear.

**David Mienczakowski (12)**
Dagfa House School, Nottingham

# Stop The War

Stop the war
It makes me bored
War is not the best
Because it is pointless
All the countries should get along
And we should sing a song.

We should all have world peace
All the big countries at least.
Maybe the small countries as well
Because all world peace has fell.

**Alexander Carr (13)**
Dagfa House School, Nottingham

# Extinction

The animals are dying
Falling to the ground
They're beginning to be extinct forever
They'll never reappear.

One animal goes down then another
Humans are left alone forever
For the animals are gone forever,
*Never* to reappear.

**David Clarke (12)**
Dagfa House School, Nottingham

# The Plague

The plague is killing the Earth
The plague is destroying the trees
The plague is killing the animals
The plague cannot be stopped
The plague will move planet to planet
The plague can never die
The plague has no cure
The plague is made of billions
The plague is mankind!

**William Naylor (12)**
Dagfa House School, Nottingham


# Oh No!

Oh no we are going to die!
Oh pollution is coming,
Oh no we are going to die!
Oh no they are destroying the ozone layer,
Oh no we are going to die unless we start to think about our Earth.

**Woo Jae Jang (12)**
Dagfa House School, Nottingham


# Click And The World's Dead

Click, one person born
Click, another person born
Click, one tree cut down
Click, another tree cut down.

One-hundred years later the population more than one billion
And the trees less than one hundred and fifty, soon it will be worse.
We need to stop what we are doing, put everything to a halt
For we are the ones who have done this and we need to fix our fault.

**Jeannie Nicolas (12)**
Dagfa House School, Nottingham

# Trees Are Cut Down For . . .

Trees are cut down for paper
Trees are cut down for wood
Trees are cut down for magazines
Trees are cut down for beds
Trees are cut down for exercise books
Trees are cut down for doors
Trees are cut down for tissues
Trees are cut down for wardrobes
What are we cut down for?

**William Merritt (12)**
Dagfa House School, Nottingham

# The Rainforest

The rainforests are red with blood
The birds are flying to their deaths
The crocodile is thirsty
The tiger is hungry
The monkeys know what we're up to.

**Tom Skill (13)**
Dagfa House School, Nottingham

# The Bee

I am just a buzzing bee
What is wrong with the world I see?
I fly around from tree to tree
But this pollution is really bugging me.
Climate change makes me sad
That honey we made was really bad.
I look at all the lovely flowers
But they're covered in litter and dirty showers.
Pollution, litter and animal extinction,
How long will I last in this country of distinction?

**Sam McMellon (12)**
Ercall Wood Technology College, Wellington

# Climate Change

C olossal temperature change
L arge atmospheric affect
I ntensity of UV rays
M elting glaciers
A rctic destruction
T itanic problems
E co-help needed fast

C arbon dioxide levels rising
H eat rise
A rctic animals at risk
N o hope left
G overnment trying their best
E co-help desperately needed.

**Steven Taras (12)**
Ercall Wood Technology College, Wellington

# The Environment

T hrough war cannot be peace
H eavy tanks of destruction
E very country should have their rights

E very animal should have their rights
N ow, today!
V iciously they are slaughtered every day
I f only violence would come to an end
R acism, a means of war and hurt
O ften violence starts through this
N ow every time you speak
M ean it before you say it
E very word, think before you say it
N ow the time has come to stop and
T hink!

**Jonathan Wilton (13)**
Ercall Wood Technology College, Wellington

# Reduce, Reuse, Recycle

Reduce, reuse, recycle
And help the environment.
Reduce the amount of litter
You throw away each day.
Recycle what you can
It's a brilliant plan,
You'll throw away less each day.

Reduce, reuse, recycle
And help the environment.
Reuse your old clothes
And you could make a bag
Or you could give them away
So on another day
Someone else could wear them.

Reduce, reuse, recycle
And help the environment.
Recycle your waste
Once a week for a year
Stop them filling holes
Make space for moles
And let tomorrow be a better day.

**Sophie Taras (12)**
Ercall Wood Technology College, Wellington

# Recycle, Reuse, Reduce

Our way of life is causing pollution
We all want to find a magic solution
Since there has not one yet been found
Everyone needs to have a good look around
From litter to carbon emissions produced
We came up with the slogan 'recycle, reuse and reduce'.

In our house we recycle everything we can
And it is collected fortnightly, by men in a van.
It makes me feel good for doing my part
Although it is small, I feel it's a start.

When I hear of rainforests being destroyed
I feel angry, upset and very annoyed.
These natural cleansers of Earth that we need
Are being chopped down and wasted, all for greed.

Global warming is the result of our way of life
For other creatures this spells trouble and strife.
From polar bears to penguins that live on the ice
They are losing their homes and paying the price.

So please do your bit and help us all
However big or small
There is still so much more I want to say
But that can wait for another day.

**Devon Birnie (12)**
Ercall Wood Technology College, Wellington

# Go Green!

Every piece of litter you drop
Means another tiring job
So put your litter in the bin
Recycle every can and tin.
Think of every single man
That comes every week inside his van.
That takes all your rubbish away
To be recycled and used another day.
Think of all the green meadows that grow the crops and you should know
All the land, farms and moor means another helpful chore.

**Rebecca Jefferson (12)**
Ercall Wood Technology College, Wellington

# Racism

Black, white, we are all the same
Everyone's in the same game.
Making money that's what we do
Name-calling doesn't matter to me or you.
Racism must come to an end
This is a message I want to send.
Let's get along, whatever we may be
Racism is wrong
Surely this you *must* see!

**Ryan Gowan (12)**
Ercall Wood Technology College, Wellington

# Litterbugs

There's a bin in every corner
No one seems to care
That's why they drop their litter
Doesn't matter where!

**Callum Barkley (12)**
Ercall Wood Technology College, Wellington

# Choices

Snap, crunch, chew
Wrappers, packets
What are you going to do?
Waiting for your first move
Your friends all around you
Cracking under the pressure
What are you going to do?
Put it in the bin and be uncool?
Drop it on the floor and be a fool?
Hold it in your hand and try to forget it?
Keep it small and drop it bit by bit
Litter isn't good
Think of the polar bears
Just remember you could
You can save the world
Take the choice.

The environment we all share
So the environment we should all care
Pollution rising
Think, what's it got to do with me?
The answer, everything!
The ice caps are melting
We need to provide sheltering
Take the chance
Stop being selfish
We're making the matter too childish
So next time you have a wrapper you can be cool
Don't mess with them icy pools
Take the choice.

**Sherie Sultana (13)**
Ercall Wood Technology College, Wellington

# Giving Animals A Chance

The world is full of animals
That sometimes we can see
But did you know that some of them
Are as rare as they can be?

Take the dolphin for example
Yangtze River is its name
I'm afraid to have to tell you
They're going as fast as they came.

I know you think that rabbits
Are as plenteous as can be
But there's one called the Rivervine
That you'll rarely ever see.

Did you enjoy looking at the rhinoceros
At the safari park last week?
Unfortunately they'll be so rare
They'll be too hard to seek.

Even pandas are endangered
Which is a shame as they're so sweet
Next time you go to China
There won't be any to meet.

The zebra with its amazing stripes
We always see at the zoo
But its vulnerability is quite great
Which is why I'm appealing to you.

The polar bear all snowy white
Soon will be extinct overnight
So we have to be very careful
And aid them in their plight.

Please think before you hunt
Or lower nets into the sea
Please give these animals a chance to live
The same chance as you'd give me.

**Elisabeth Brewer (13)**
Ercall Wood Technology College, Wellington

# The Future

Look into the future
About one hundred years
With talking turkeys
And jumping deer.
Are we going to see them
Talking and jumping
If we carry on? Emm!
No! If we carry on dumping.
There's a magical place
Beyond the front gate
Over the concrete lace
Just take your mate.
There are fields of flowers
Beyond our front gates
Just use your powers
And don't be late.
Penguins and polar bears
Are wonderful things
You just have to care
And they'll show off their blings.
Humans are the cause
In our homes
Open some doors
And use our bones.
We can make a difference, now we can
Just try your hardest and join in the fun.

**Summer Davies-Newton & Sophie Berry (12)**
Ercall Wood Technology College, Wellington

# Litter Is Bad

Litter is bad if you know what I mean
We just want our streets to be really clean.
When people drop litter they think that it's cool
But really, they are just great big fools.
It's wrecking our environment, can't you see?
Lots of people hate it, including me.
So use the bins provided, it's the only way,
So don't drop litter, it wrecks the day.

**Mitchell Brassington (13)**
Ercall Wood Technology College, Wellington

# Recycling

R ubbish is what our world creates
E nvironmental impact is what that makes
C reating less waste is the way
Y ou and me need to reduce our waste and
   help save our planet today
C ardboard, paper, glass and tins
L et's put them in their special bins
I ndividual clothing we recycle too
N eedy people will think they're new
G etting people all involved
   Save our planet, problem solved.

**Paige Mitchell (12)**
Ercall Wood Technology College, Wellington

# Save The Earth

We will die
The world and I
If we can't save the Earth.
Recycle cans and clothes and pens
It could start from birth.
If we work together
To tie the sever
We could save the world
So use your red boxes
Not for the foxes
And save this world.

**Laura Henighan (13)**
Ercall Wood Technology College, Wellington

# Will?

Will I be able to drive a car that is not poisonous?
Will I be able to write on a piece of paper?
Will there be any trees left to make paper?
Will there be enough coal to run power stations?
Will there be enough power stations to make electricity?
Will there still be poverty?
Will there be people on the streets who are homeless?
Will my future kids be able to write in books at school?
Will my kids be able to read books?
Will my kids be able to play in the snow?
Will my kids be bullied at school?
Will we have to hear racist comments as we walk around?
Will countries still go to war to get what they want?
Will there be any animals that I have seen when I have been to the zoo?
Will there be forests and places for these animals to live in?
Will we have to walk on a wasteland instead of a nice clean pathway?

I wouldn't have to ask these questions if we changed the way we treat our environment!

**Charlotte Eggerton (13)**
Ercall Wood Technology College, Wellington

# Recycling Rap

Listen to me people, hear what I say,
We've got to start recycling, it's the only way.
To save this planet for future generations
The name of the game is reclamation.
You've got to start recycling; you know it makes sense,
You've got to start recycling, stop sitting on the fence.
No more pussyfooting, no more claptrap,
Get yourself doing the recycling rap.

Come on and start recycling, start today
By saving old newspaper not throwing it away.
Don't just take them and dump them on the tip
Tie them in a bundle and take them to the skip.
Get collecting; protecting the future is up to you
Save all your glass bottles and your jam jars too
Take them to the bottle bank and then to the factory
The glass can be recycled, saving energy.
Don't chuck away that empty can
Remember what I said, start recycling man.
Wash it, squash it and squeeze it flat and thin
And post it therein.

Listen to me people, hear what I say
We've got to start recycling, it's the only way
To save this planet for future generations
The name of the game is reclamation.
You've got to start recycling, you know it makes sense
You've got to start recycling, stop sitting on the fence.
No more pussyfooting, no more claptrap,
Get yourself doing the recycling rap.

**Shahneela Khan (12)**
Ercall Wood Technology College, Wellington

# Homelessness

As I wander around town at the end of the day
I'm tired but happy in a strange kind of way.
I'm just thinking of how lucky it is
That I have a safe warm place, this I used to miss
When I was younger my family could not cope without any money
All they could do was hope.
I lived without a home for half a year
And during that time I was in fear, now I'm back on track
We still shudder when we think about all those years back.

**Holly Cowperthwaite (11)**
Harris School, Rugby

# Stop The War

For all the fired guns and scattered bodies,
Broken hearts and growing poppies.
For the agony suffered,
The lives lost,
Family and friends,
Their bodies tossed.
The war is bad,
The war is sad,
It makes some cry,
But the others mad.
So let's stop the war,
Put it to an end,
And let all the world be one big friend.

**George Dixon (11)**
Harris School, Rugby

# Unfortunate Creatures

Climate change melting the ice
Flooding many animals, killing mice
Climate change endangers many others
Melting ice into water
Destroying every house of polar bears
Enraging them, polar bears' tempers flare
The penguins act the same
Pollution everywhere
The *human race* is to blame.

**Callum Brewerton (11)**
Harris School, Rugby

# My Relatives

To be an eco-warrior on this planet
You don't want to be like my auntie Janet.
All she does is sit in a chair
She doesn't think and she doesn't care.
She doesn't recycle and leaves her litter in the park
And she's nothing like my uncle Mark.

My uncle Mark is really green
He wants this planet to be nice and clean.
He collects all his cardboard and saves all his tins
Then takes them along to the recycling bins.

But the biggest issue is global warming
And frankly I find it rather boring
Because even though I'm an eco-kid
I'd rather be like my cousin Sid.

My cousin, he is the best
He doesn't worry or get stressed.
He doesn't think he's a one-man-band
But he likes everyone to lend a hand.

So let's just try and work together
And save this planet forever and ever.
Let's live in peace and stop the war
Let's love our neighbour and feed the poor.

**Michael Kearney (11)**
Harris School, Rugby

# War Is Nobody's Friend

Blood soaks the floor
Children driven from their homes
Men and women all lifeless on the floor
Children call it the war game but this is no game
People are dying, children are crying
How did it start, how will it end?
War is nobody's friend.

Landmines make nowhere safe
Mortars wreck the land
Green fields turn to red
Bombers destroy all that we have
It is our war, so why is the Earth suffering?
How did it start, how will it end?
War is nobody's friend.

**Mathew Lewis (11)**
Harris School, Rugby

# Wondering

I sit here wondering, wondering what my fate would be
But now it's easy to see, deforestation is taking over me.
I'm scared to death!
Will someone tell me what will happen next?
They're chopping down the trees and killing lots of species
*Help!* Here come the humans in those big machines.
My mum keeps telling me along with the trees
Our species stands no chance but the humans *will* advance.
Small animals like us, we can't make a fuss
Our lives are in your hands, please help us
Stop your plans!

**Bethany Mackintosh (11)**
Harris School, Rugby

# War

War is poverty and death
War should never happen
War is terrible
War is sadness
War smells like mouldy cheese
War looks like your worst nightmare
War feels like mud
War tastes like lemons
War is hatred
War is pain
War is unhappiness
War is jealousy.

**Connor Nichols (11)**
Harris School, Rugby

# Recycle, Save The World

To make the world a better place
Please try and recycle all of your waste.
Instead of making the landfill bigger
Try and recycle all your litter.
If you enjoy climbing trees
Make sure they're not cut down please.
Metal, card, paper, plastic
Saving the world makes you feel fantastic.
Take things out of the bin
Put them in the recycling.
A better world this would produce
If only you would reuse, recycle, reduce.

**Hannah Palmer (12)**
Harris School, Rugby

# Animal Testing

When we buy a new product do we ever stop to think
About the animals in testing, what do they think?
It's all because of lipliner, lipgloss or lipbalm
It's tried on the animals which cause them harm
How are manufacturers sure we're safe to use it?
It the animal doesn't die get a disease or sue them.

**Shannon Crowe (11)**
Harris School, Rugby

# Litter Is Bitter

Litter is bitter because it's killing animals,
So having fags is still bad,
Think of the animals which are eating your litter.
How would you like it, eating your litter?
So dropping litter is a dangerous thing.

**Daniel Marshall (11)**
Harris School, Rugby

# Rainforests

When we sit at school writing in our book
Just give it a second look
*Paper!* Rainforests are cut down day by day
And cause destruction, they should pay!
Animals dying because of this,
Can you tell me more please Miss?

**Elouise Merryweather (11)**
Harris School, Rugby

# The World Should Be A Tidy Place

Cars, motorbikes, planes cause pollution
There is one big solution
Cut down on your $CO_2$
That applies to the world, me and you.
Recycle paper, plastic, glass and cans
Show the world we are first class.
Do not waste electricity, gas and water
As this will keep your bills shorter.
Keep your world a tidy place
So the children can enjoy the space.

**Manpreet Sidhu (11)**
Harris School, Rugby

# No TV

You should not watch TV
It's destroying our world, do you not see
What our world can be without TV?
So everyone would go outside and have more pride
In the whole world wide.

**Charlie Reed (11)**
Harris School, Rugby

# Racism

Black, green, red or blue
The colour of someone's skin should matter to you.
You hurt their feelings down inside
So maybe next time you should think with your mind.
Now let's all be kind, don't judge someone's race or looks or what you read in
papers also books
For a kind heart is what is favoured.

**Suzanne Hilton (11)**
Harris School, Rugby

# Keep It Green!

Recycle less, recycle more
You can even recycle your own front door.
Recycling your greens is good
It puts the nutrients back into the mud.
You can recycle paper, cans and plastic
It's truly fantastic.
Recycling can be fun
It can be done in the sun.
You recycle your garden waste
To improve your veggies' taste.
So please be smart and keep it green
And help our planet to be clean.

**Gemma Scales (11)**
Harris School, Rugby

# Recycle To Save The World

If we don't recycle the world will disappear.
If we don't switch lights off the world will disappear!
Can't you spare your time just to put a glass bottle in your red box?
Please recycle for the world's sake.

**Connor Callan (11)**
Harris School, Rugby

# Paper

Paper, paper, don't use lots of paper
The trees will go and we will die
So don't use lots of paper.
The paper we have we need to look after,
The trees we use we need to look after.
Where is our life when we use all this paper?

**Bethany Grace Barnes (11)**
Harris School, Rugby

# War Going On, Where Do I Go?

War going on, where do I go?
Running, running for shelter
Hoping that we will not be killed.
Screams, screams are all around us.
Help us; help us, give us some love,
Isn't there somebody out there?
Worried, scared, frightened, what's going to happen next?
War going on, where do I go?

**Gemma Dez-la-Lour (11)**
Harris School, Rugby

# Environmentally Friendly

Red, blue, green, every colour to be seen
How we sort our rubbish every day
Mass recycling underway.
Paper, cardboard, tins and cans
Our local council has big plans
Whatever it is, we throw away
It will be recycled from today!

**Toby Mearns (11)**
Harris School, Rugby

# By The Minute

What's happening to our world?
It's getting weaker and it's your fault.
It will get darker by the year and smellier by the month.
Filthier by the day, more uncomfortable by the hour,
Polluted by the minute and destroyed second by second.
How will our kids live in a world like this
They won't be thanking us, they will hate us.

**Karoline Leite (11)**
Harris School, Rugby

# The Big Green Machine, This Is What It Does

Recycle me and wait and see
What you get back from me.

Make a pencil pot from a tin
Don't put it in the bin.

There is lots to save
So please behave
Recycle now
You know how.

The rainforests we see
Our children won't
Teach all to recycle
And help those who don't.

Animals need our help
They are becoming extinct quick
So please everyone, recycle!

**Jack Hale (12)**
Harris School, Rugby

# Make The World A Better Place

We litter,
We destroy rainforests,
We bring war,
We kill animals,
We do everything,
We are racist,
We kill people,
We never bring peace to the world,
We pollute the air but now it is time for me to say stop, *stop!*
Stop the litter, the animal cruelty and help the world be a better place.

**Chloe Mitchell (11)**
Harris School, Rugby

# Recycle

R is for recycle tins, cans, paper, bottles and garden waste
E is for eco, to be friendly to our planet
C is for clutter, if you don't need it, lose it
Y is for you, you can help
C is for climate change, turn off that standby button
L is for landfill sites where we put too much of our rubbish
E is for everyone can save the planet.

**Emma Tiffany Ruth Lenton (11)**
Harris School, Rugby

# Being Green

To keep the world green you must be clean.
And making pollution is not the solution.
If you drop litter you are just bitter
Don't take a bus or a car
Get on a bike and you will go far.
Recycle, recycle, a message from Michael
Keep the world clean so we can be green.

**Michael Fletcher-Fathers (11)**
Harris School, Rugby

# Earth

Stop pollution, stop litter because the world is at risk and you are to blame.
Racism, war is wore than before.
Litter, pollution, what's the solution?
Rainforest burning, burning till they're gone
So come on, before the world has gone.

**Rebecca Roberts (12)**
Harris School, Rugby

# Recycling

Use less throttles
Reuse more bottles.
Crushed cans
Can make pans.
Old scrap wood
Can be reused, oh yes ít should.

Pollution
Unattended television
Sends my dad into devastation!
Lightbulbs left on
Electricity bills go on and on.
Increasing bills and gas
Oh dear, no cash.

Animals' extinction
The forests are going
What's next, is it the dolphins?
By recycling down on the farm
We do less harm.
We need to help the struggling bees
By doing the garden, we get sore knees.

**Aidan Dolman (11)**
Harris School, Rugby

# Gorillas

G orillas are becoming extinct
O r can we help to stop this?
R ainforests are being cut down
I f this continues the gorillas will
L ose their habitat
L eave them alone
A nd stop cutting down their home
S o that they can live on.

**Jaymie Batchelor (11)**
Harris School, Rugby

# Being Homeless

Nowhere to go
Nowhere to know
No bed
No clothes
No shower
Nowhere to go
Just keep wandering
No clean clothes
Smell dirty
Horrible
I haven't even got a comb
So that's me
No home.

**Daniel Howells (12)**
Harris School, Rugby

# Pollution

Every day, every hour
People make pollution
Maybe one day
We can find a solution.

We make it working in industry
We make it when we drive
We make it when we go on trains
We need to step back and take five.

We can find cleaner fuels
We can use cars less
If everyone makes more effort
We can save our planet, oh yes!

**Thomas Barnett (11)**
Harris School, Rugby

# On The Brink Of Extinction

Cold, damp towering forests in which pandas lay.
Pandas eat bamboo not long bristly hay.
Born in groups of three, all night and day the young ones play.
China is their natural home but zoos will soon be where they stay.

**Eleanor Hudson (11)**
Harris School, Rugby

# Our Cruel World

The world is fragile
The world is ours
To care for and look after
As best as we can.

The animals we love
The animals we care about
Are in danger from us
Why did we do it?

**Susannah Scattergood (12)**
Harris School, Rugby

# Being Homeless

'I am OK'
I say to myself when I wake up in the middle of the night all alone
'I am OK'
I say to myself you are not at home, you are in the street all alone but don't cry,
you will be OK.
'I am OK'
I am doing what I can to be brave and strong and to survive
Until then I say to myself, 'I am OK.'

**Natasha Cottrell (11)**
Harris School, Rugby

# A Touch Of Destruction

Another day to try and find some food or water to survive on.
The homeless and poor walk back to nothing
A little pile of sticks and mud, maybe a shelter for a day.
*Smash!* Another block of Arctic ice hitting the water
As the sun beats down on a place that is meant to be ice-cold.
No water and a dusty desert drying up
Getting crispy hot as the sun sizzles the sand.
*Whoosh!* Water flooding towns and villages because of rising sea levels.
The world has a big effect from man-made pollution
Which ruins the atmosphere, which protects all from the sun.
You gave the Earth an impact like never before
So it's giving us a deadly warning and it's taking effect already.
Damage, destruction, extinction of animals, do your bit, save the planet.

**Sasha Fellowes (12)**
Harris School, Rugby

# Recycle

R  is for reduce, reuse, recycle
E  is for environment
C  is for recycle cans and card
Y  is for you're welcome to help
C  is for everything you recycle will count
L  is for learning to do it
E  is for everyone can help.

**Aimee Martin (11)**
Harris School, Rugby

# An End To War

When I think of war I think of . . .
People dying,
Jets flying,
Guns shooting,
Robbers looting,
Bombs exploding,
Tanks reloading,
There is sadness and badness,
Where there should be gladness
There goes death.
Soldiers take their last breath.
There is so much pain,
People die in vain,
Piece by piece the peace returns.
But how does the war end?
There's a change of mind and heart
And diplomacy starts
Shadows are disappearing
Happiness is reappearing.

**Adam Low (11)**
Harris School, Rugby

# Rainforests

Rainforests are green
Some animals inside are mean
Parts have died and turned brown
Because people are cutting them down.
I think they should stop
And we should be on top
So the animals will be safe.

**Jordan Murray (11)**
Harris School, Rugby

# Homeless People

The homeless are ill
With nowhere to go
No sleep, no food,
No clothes too.

They are abused
With no one to go to,
Humiliated in front of strangers.
Who can help them?

A cardboard box
Is there mansion.
Be grateful for what you have got
Don't abuse it.

Disease killing them,
They need warmth.
If we don't help
They'll be doomed!

They can't afford anything
Not even a penny sweet.
They don't have a birthday or Christmas
They just want a life.

**Kane Gayle (11)**
Harris School, Rugby

# The Environment

If you want to be green
You have to be mean.
You cannot waste all the things we do
Just think twice
Make sure you're nice
And don't throw so much away.

**Luke Norman (11)**
Harris School, Rugby

# Animal Extinction

A nimals are becoming extinct
N ot enough people care.
I t's an opinion that I don't share.
M any people wonder why they're there
A nd I think more people should be made aware.
L et's do our best to show we care.

E verybody has a part to play
X tinction should not be the way.
T reat animals kind and fair
I n a way that shows you care.
N ow be kind to our planet
'C ause our future is dependent on it.
T o make sure the creatures are here to see
I n their defence we need to be.
O ur animals are a natural attraction
N ow is the time to all take some action.

**Sophie Lunn (11)**
Harris School, Rugby

# Recycle Your Waste

Recycle recycle
Don't throw it away
Save the planet
For another day.

Recycle recycle
Don't waste that paper
It takes trees to make it
So reuse it later.

Recycle recycle
Your plastic, paper and glass
Help to keep the planet
Covered in trees and lush green grass.

**Ben Williamson (12)**
Harris School, Rugby

# Need A Solution

Pollution
Needs a solution
Quick - fast
Or this world will not last.

Pollution
Needs a solution.
Wise - keen
Please keep our world clean.

Pollution
Needs a solution.
Prompt - clever
Or else lose this world forever.

Pollution
Needs a solution
Needs it now!

**Harry Williamson (11)**
Harris School, Rugby

# The Environment

Don't leave rubbish on the floor
Pick it up or much more
Never spit your chewing gum
It will stick to the floor
It might seem that it isn't much
But everything you do is to help the environment.

**Sophie Winham (11)**
Harris School, Rugby

# World Emotions

Emotions can be happy,
Emotions can be sad.
Emotions can be good,
Emotions can be bad.
Emotions are around us every single day
Emotions are around us in every single way.

When animals' homes are being destroyed they can't help but be annoyed.
People in wars can get killed by a bullet but they feel more than pain
They feel more than anger, they feel more than sadness
Before they drop to the floor like their legs are no more.
When we recycle we feel we've done our part
But we also feel happiness in our heart.
We need emotions to live in this world
To look after it and to keep it the way it is.
Not hotter, not colder, the world should stay as it is!
But each of us needs a heart so we can play our part
Emotions can be happy,
Emotions can be sad.

**Joseph Craggs (12)**
Higham Lane School, Nuneaton

# The Endless War

Screaming bellows from the streets,
*Boom!*
Children running,
Shots firing,
Bullets penetrating,
*Boom!*
Screams, 'Help me,' a man cries.
'The endless war,' the wise man said.
*Boom!*

**Ian Ensor (12)**
Higham Lane School, Nuneaton

# Our Climate

O ur lives are full of selfishness
U nderestimating what the power of Mother Nature can do to us
R ealising that our lives are at stake

C limate changing at a rapid rate
L ives will be lost if something is not done
I magine that, a world with no one on
M any are starting to change their ways
A ll must change otherwise it'll be our final days
T ime is ticking, our existence is on edge
E volution will end, surely this isn't our pledge?

**James Cox (12)**
Higham Lane School, Nuneaton

# The Future Of Earth Is In Our Hands

In the future our Earth may not be the same.
The towering roaring monsters of the waves,
The godforsaken, overhanging leafless branches for trees,
The new damp, murky green smog of a sky,
The annihilation of the Earth could be just around the corner
And all we are doing is helping it on its way.
Mysterious putrid fumes ascend from our factories' chimneys into the sky,
Our repulsive toxic waste foams into the sea,
Foul debris from our houses piles into loathsome landfill sites.
The world is changing under our noses, if we want change it should happen now
Else this extraordinary planet will die knowing its own people killed it.

**Owen Woodward (12)**
Higham Lane School, Nuneaton

# Animal Extinction

I thought the world was caring
I thought we stuck together
Fur is what the celebs are wearing
Will the animals be safe forever?

The problem won't stop growing
As the day goes by
But can you go on knowing
They'll become extinct and die?

Some of their homes are cut down
Some are taken away
Animals left feeling down
As it happens every day.

We've got to stop
We've got to stop now
Before the problem reaches the top
Do well and take a bow.

**Rhian Ingram (12)**
Higham Lane School, Nuneaton

# Pollution Needs A Solution

Mother Earth is a special planet
Nothing can go wrong on it, or can it?
The way things are going
There's no way of knowing
If we're heading for a crisis
That could be decisive
Can Mother Earth survive
To keep us all alive?

**Dawn Haffner (12)**
Higham Lane School, Nuneaton

# War Around Me

I look around, evidence of war everywhere.
On the television, on the Internet,
On games and in books.
All including death, sorrow, sadness,
Hate and forgiveness, victory and defeat.
But why is there war
And can it be stopped?

**Bradley Parrott (13)**
Higham Lane School, Nuneaton

# Who's Next?

Tigers and rhinos nearly gone
Shot by mean poachers
Hunted for their claws, horns and fur.

The dodo's gone, not one left.
Who will be the next?
Will it be the lion maybe?

Soon there will be only us left,
Is that what you want
A barren world with only us?

**Matthew Osborne (12)**
Higham Lane School, Nuneaton

# The Grass Is Green

The grass is green and the skies are blue
It's better this way for me and you.
When the grass is brown and the skies are black
You'll be wanting your old world back
So start right now to save the planet
And I promise you won't regret it.

**Josie Kaya Garner (12)**
Higham Lane School, Nuneaton

# Lying In The Dark

Homeless is what they call them
Because they have no home
They live their lives on the streets
And choose to drift and roam.

We say they choose this lonely life
And to live alone
They rest below the stars at night
And live out on their own.

They often beg for food
Or steal from a house
But all they have for company
Is a timid little mouse.

How do they live like this
Falling asleep in a park
Bundled up in a jacket
Lying in the dark?

**Christie Moreton (12)**
Higham Lane School, Nuneaton

# Mother Nature's Cry

The bold blues from the river burned to brown
We hear aeroplanes flying
Although the trees are silently dying.
Rainforests shrinking
The homes of animals being taken away
But they never have a chance to say, *stop!*
Stop taking our lives, our homes,
The trees are not yours to own.
All Mother Nature can do is sit and sigh as she asks, why?
Why, why must mankind cause the world to die?
You'd think we'd learn as time passes by.

**Tara Kaur Sarkaria (12)**
Higham Lane School, Nuneaton

# When I Look Around I See . . .

When I look around I see . . .
Man turning on man
Killing with devastating devices of death
No one alters their aim
As they must stick to the battle plan.

When I look around I see . . .
The smell of rotting flesh swirls around and around
Fire blazing in and out
An evil burning core lies in every mortal
Sections of decapitated body litters the ground.

When I look around I see . . .
Citizens suffering, having to pay for the killing machines
Children's minds being poisoned with visions of war
Depressing the souls of many with images of things being smashed into
smithereens

When I look around I hope to see . . .
Things changing, individuals speaking out
Leaders listening and making the right decisions.
And the message sinking in
As a whisper can mean more than a shout

When you look around, what do *you* see?

**Ruth Phillips (13)**
Higham Lane School, Nuneaton

# Town Of Disgrace

We will help this town of disgrace
For people in need, pollution and wars taking place.

Don't chuck litter in that bin
Recycle it instead of just wasting
It's bad to not reuse and throw it on the floor
We've got to help this town and so much more.

We will help this town of disgrace
For people in need, pollution and wars taking place.

Help the homeless sleep somewhere safe
The street is not good for a sleeping place
Say no to racism and treat everyone the same
No one's the same so there's no one to blame.

We will help this town of disgrace
For people in need, pollution and wars taking place.

Think of all the animals extinct right now
Damaging their homes by using a plough
Just think of that paper and card you use
So next time someone says, 'Chuck this in the bin,' just refuse.

We will help this town of disgrace
For people in need, pollution and wars taking place.

Help the world be better today
By recycling and reusing on your way.

**Georgia Goodman (11)**
Higham Lane School, Nuneaton

# Environment

E veryone's responsible
N obody cares
V ulnerable animals suffer
I raq soldiers defend
R acism affects the young
O ld women scared to speak
N obody cares
M en with axes cut down trees
E veryone's to blame
N obody cares
T orture.

**Jamie Taylor (12)**
Higham Lane School, Nuneaton

# Why?

When this world was made
It was all so neat and clean
So why must mankind be so mean?
The sea was flowing so free
So why did we not let it be?
The wind was so calm and fresh
So why let it get into this awful mess?
Why turn your world upside down
If it only makes people moan and frown.

**Ashleigh Newton (12)**
Higham Lane School, Nuneaton

# I Don't Like Our Weather

I don't like global warming
I hate that it's always storming
I don't like air pollution
What is the solution?
I don't like cold weather
I hate it as it makes me shiver
I don't like weather revolutions
What are the solutions?

**Saminder Dehill (12)**
Higham Lane School, Nuneaton

# Bitter Litter

I have made this rhyme
To talk about a serious crime
Which has a fine
I would not like to be mine.

Its name is litter
Which is oh so bitter
From sweet wrappers to fags
And cans to bags.

Meaning more pollution
And this is the solution
Start to recycle
And ride your bicycle.

**Thomas Bourne (12)**
Higham Lane School, Nuneaton

# Rainforest Frown

The rainforests are being cut down
That makes the people frown
The water in the forests will not flow
Because the people are feeling low.

Chop, chop, down goes the tree
The chopper only cares for himself
What food will later go in his mouth
Not caring about his health.

Without the Amazon we won't survive
We will be having no living alive
People in the forest will die
So that's why we must try
Try to save the world today
This is what I propose to say
Don't let people chop trees down
Turn around that horrible frown
Make the frown into a smile
Don't let the trees go on trial
Join a charity to save the trees
Don't let them cry
You too can save them, if only you try.

**Lydia Ellis (12)**
Higham Lane School, Nuneaton

# Pollution

P eople are panicking
O verreacting
L ots of rubbish just
L eft anywhere
U seless appliances left anywhere
T housands more
I deas needed
O r else
N othing can be done.

**Josh Guilfoyle (12)**
Higham Lane School, Nuneaton

# Tick-Tock

Brum, brum, tick-tock
They infuriate the city
They fill the world with pity
Day by day
More are sold
They're causing fear
They're ending the world
Brum, brum, tick-tock
*Crash!*

Drip-drop, tick-tock
The coldest place
Is the end of the race
Day by day
They float away
They're causing fear

They're ending the world
Drip-drop, tick-tock
*Gone!*

Both of these things
Are the cause of each other
So tell your father and your mother
There are many heroes and you could be one
Save the world and walk!

**Rebecca Painter (12)**
Higham Lane School, Nuneaton

# Earth's Murderer

P ollution
O zone layer destroyed
L ife dying
L evel of water rising
U K floods
T rees killed
I ce caps falling
O xygen repaired with $CO_2$
N ot too late, save the planet.

**Dylan Drewitt (13)**
Higham Lane School, Nuneaton

# Global Warming

Global warming is at the door
A problem increasing more and more.
Global warming is blocking our way
We need your help to keep it at bay.

Global warming is our downfall
The world needs a wake-up call.
With all our strength we will fight
To save our planet day and night.

Every day we cause pollution
Let's start searching for the solution.
The three Rs should be put to use
Recycle, reduce and reuse.

Don't take a bath, take a shower
Help save energy, water and power.
Use the paths and not the roads
This will decrease the problem loads.

Global warming is on our doormat
Help save an animal's habitat.
The arising problem should be seen
Let's colour our country, make it green.

Global warming is at the door
A problem increasing, more and more.
Global warming is blocking our way
We need *your* help to keep it at bay.

**Nicola Bowen (12)**
Higham Lane School, Nuneaton

# The Green Machine's Big Battle

The fine pine bristles whisper in the gale
We would want to see these bristles all fall down and fail
And look towards the brown body on which it stands so tall
'Let us cut these down,' I say and laugh as they fall.

The leaves of those that live grand lives
Why should we watch as this beast thrives
And the roots so majestic run though the ground
Let us burn them all I say, so they can't be found.
The rumbling in the forest draws closer
No one ever dares say, 'No sir'
Your brothers fall like twigs in the wind
Let us come and treat them as binned.

The dust settles and the battle is decided
They have won but have not subsided.
They carry on like water in a river
Eating away at the great forest's liver.

**Callum Luke Garnham (12)**
Higham Lane School, Nuneaton

# Poverty

Poverty is bad, the homeless are sad
Children alone, barely a bone
No food, no wealth and so little health.
It's hard to survive below the poverty line.

Children cry as their families die
From unknown diseases, they hope their life eases
If the richer could see that just a small fee
Could really prevent pain and poverty.

**Cara Sutton (12)**
Higham Lane School, Nuneaton

# The Philosophy Of Planet Earth

What is this philosophy?
What does the future hold for me?
Trees scream as we kill them
So wipe off the trees' frown
Stop creating mayhem
And stop cutting them down.

Do you care about nature?
Tweety birds too?
To save a poor creature
It's all down to you.

White is black, black is white
Big and thin are just the same
Tall and small, they're both right
Everyone's in the same game.

War, poverty, racism too
Surely it's just best to be kind.
Do you want it to happen to you?
If so, you're out of your mind!

Credit crunch creeps up, it's a catastrophe
People are as poor as a church mouse without any cheese.
Why is everything a philosophy?
Gordon Brown, Prime Minister, stop this credit crunch please!
What is this philosophy?
What does the future hold for me?

**Amelia Tarling (12)**
Higham Lane School, Nuneaton

# Why?

Your perception is wrong; I'm not what you see
All you are doing is preventing me, me.
I try to be different to just hide my pain
But you think I'm weird because I'm not the same.
You make me feel rubbish and put me in fear
It's happened to me year after year.
I hate what you're doing, it's making me cry
What I am saying simply is, why?

**Daniel Hodges (12)**
Higham Lane School, Nuneaton

# Endangered Environment

E veryone should recycle and war should stop
N obody should litter or pollute
V ery big climate changes are happening
I ndeed everyone can help and work together
R ainforests are being chopped down
O ur future should be good not bad
N ot everyone has a home but should
M ore and more poverty is going on
E xtinction of animals is happening
N ot everyone has a bed
T ry not to litter but recycle instead.

**Georgia Hadley (12)**
Higham Lane School, Nuneaton

# Pollution - Do And Die!

Do you want to breathe again?
If yes then say and fight among the tears and pain
To find an answer, to find the end.

One way to change, if you want to stop your driving
Get a bike or start to walk
There's an answer, walk, walk, walk!

Stop pollution, then you breathe
Stop pollution and then live for evermore
Just *stop!*

Turn off your PlayStation
Turn off your oven
If you do then you govern how you live
And how the world thrives and thrives and thrives.

**Philip Potts (12)**
Higham Lane School, Nuneaton

# Why Do They Do It?

Every day more animals die from poachers who kill for money.
If only they knew what they were really doing.
Destroying wildlife here and there, destroying more everywhere.
Even though there is a rule, poachers don't care, money is too important to them.
If only they could care about these poor animals
Then some of them might still be alive.

**William Woods (12)**
Higham Lane School, Nuneaton

# Extinction Is Forever

Extinction is forever
They will never come back
They're wiped off the planet
That's so out of whack.

Many kingdoms
Have stood before,
But what was decided?
Were they just a bore?

They roamed the Earth as well
Don't they have a choice
Whether they should live or not?
Why don't we all rejoice!

We are surrounded
By many incredible things
We are happy with these wonders on our planet
So let's all dance and sing.

We have lived for thousands of years
In peace with all these creatures
So why does this have to end now?
When was all this decided?

Hate is shot through metal contraptions
But love is fired through care
Let's stop the hunters with their guns
And start the endangered's care.

What happened to all the love
We were so happy to give?
Long ago it was up to them
But now it's up to us!

**Harry King (11)**
Higham Lane School, Nuneaton

# Green Is The Colour Our World Should Be

Green is the colour our world should be
Blue is the colour of our sky
Orange is the colour of our glistening sun
And grey are the planes as they pass me by.

Silver is the colour of the shining stars
Red are the leaves that fall from the trees
Yellow is the colour of the sand on the beach
And black is the colour of the hardworking bees.

Brown is the earth beneath my feet
Bright is the morning light
Dark are the rain clouds above my head
And white is the colour of the wolves that fight.

Green is the colour our world should be
Blue is the colour of our sky
Orange is the colour of our glistening sun
And grey are the planes as they pass me by.

Let us try and keep it this way
Or we can all say goodbye
To the magical planet that we call Earth
In the midst of this enormous universe.

**Rebecca Amos-Hirst (13)**
Higham Lane School, Nuneaton

# Racism

Yo, yo, yo, what do we have here?
Different colour, race, so close and so near.
But why is it a problem, what do we all have to face,
Why can't we all run the same kinda race?

Everyone is different, what's the problem with that?
Why can't everyone stick together, can anyone see
We're all the same on the inside just like you and me?

Yo, yo, yo, how can we fix the matter?
People's lives are nothing like chandeliers that shatter.
Everyone is a colour so they have no right to be
Spiteful, aggressive to others, can't anyone see?

You don't have to be racist just to be cool
But being racist just makes you a fool.
Don't judge people by their colour and their skin,
Carry on like this and you'll never win.

Yo, yo, yo, get yourself out of this mess
Just give it all up and try your best.
Why don't we just try and stick together
Keep everyone smiling now and forever.

**Muneebah Hafejee (11)**
Higham Lane School, Nuneaton

# Keep Your Eyes Open

Take a look at the suffering
People's hearts broken
Never to be put together again.

Take a look at the suffering
Their hunger is dying
Sometimes lucky if they get a seed.

Take a look at the suffering
Those who suffer from diseases
That could be cured elsewhere
Dying down slowly, slowly to the end.

If the world just gave one penny, just one,
It would give those who suffer
A better place to live
Keep your eyes open, always.

**Sim Johal (12)**
Higham Lane School, Nuneaton

# A Bullet's Been Shot, I Wish It Had Not!

Every day people die
Through the air screams and bullets fly.
Children always living in fear
It's become normal to shed a tear,
Even though war comes and goes
It always makes more widows.
With all this blood being shed
More and more families aren't being fed.
Every day children dream of going to schools
In war there are no playground rules.
That's what war is, out of hand,
War is in the forest, sea, snow and sand.
Either way it is death that stalks the land
I only have one question and it is for those who die,
Even though it doesn't sound like much, I just want to know
  Why?

**Logan Ryan (12)**
Higham Lane School, Nuneaton

# What Is It To You?

Long ago
When dinosaurs roamed
When pterodactyls sat
On their mountain top home.
The animals got along
No poverty or strife
No unfairness and meanness
Just the natural long life.
We started spoiling the world
Swallow your pride
Open your eyes
To the suffering outside.
Stop polluting and wasting
Give kindness and scope
Stop poverty and wars
Give love and much hope.
The grass is green
The sea is blue
This is the world
What is it to you?

**Jasmin Rees (11)**
Higham Lane School, Nuneaton

# No More War

There are a lot of people poor
And some of that is down to war.
War is horrid, very bad,
Leaving many people sad.
The bullets howl and they shrill
Whizzing along with intent to kill.
Don't go to war, it is no fun,
There is nothing great about a gun.
Earth is going round the bend
Somehow, some way it has to end.
It is not good, it is not clever
It can't go on forever and ever.

**Alex Thorne (12)**
Higham Lane School, Nuneaton

# Forget Racism 'Cause You're Unique

Why does racism exist?
To be cool you don't have to be racist.
Everyone in this world is unique,
Forget joining some silly clique.

Being different is like a talent
Why be ashamed of your accent, colour or race?
What's the difference?
It's like we're all the same face to face.

There's no rule in the rule book
Saying about how you should look.
Who's saying someone doesn't like you?
No one, that's who!

Be proud of what you are,
Being disappointed won't get you far.
No matter what's all around you
Being who you are will get you through.

**Ammaarah Hafejee (13)**
Higham Lane School, Nuneaton

# The Dying World

The sky of a bright electric blue glances down at the Earth in pain,
It cries and wails as the thick evil poison slowly kills it.
The polar bear, valiant and bold, collapses in exhaustion.
Its winter wonderland slowly getting eaten away.
Open your eyes to the suffering, the world is crying out for help.
Let the fortunate help the unfortunate and the unfortunate to be fortunate
Help make our wondrous world a better place and don't let the hunters
become the hunted.

**Luke Griffin (11)**
Higham Lane School, Nuneaton

# Pollution - The Car's Perspective

*Chug*
*Chug*
*Chug*
Along the busy main road I go
Weaving in and out of the cars
I can smell the pollution in the air
Rising up into the clouds
But nobody seems to care.

They all still drive around
Not thinking twice about the damage they're causing
People blame it on me
But they don't realise what they're doing
Polluting the environment, don't you see?

*Chug*
*Chug*
*Chug*
I keep on going
They drive on and on
Radio loud
Global warming it says
I hope they're not proud.

Red light
Engine still going
*Pollution*
*Pollution*
*Pollution!*

**Mollie Watkins (12)**
Higham Lane School, Nuneaton

# Free

Take a look around
What do you see?
People who are happy and full of glee
No!
All we see is punishment and crime
Country by country fighting through time.

People in Zimbabwe
No drink or food to eat
If we unite the world, together, it can be beat.
All together hand in hand
Without Hitler or Hussein
Tears flood the nation as they reign.

Wars are starting
Wars are ending
By staying together we can keep defending
The right to be free!

**Chloe Hood (12)**
Higham Lane School, Nuneaton

# Strange

Strange.
You think of the most irrelevant things when you're about to die.
What about when you're about to kill someone else?
The first kill is the worst probably, I wouldn't know.
The thought of all the irrelevant thoughts flying around a field
For a point of politics is more painful
Then the bullets that drive through shoulders and skulls.
War. Strange.

**Andrew Bilbie (12)**
Higham Lane School, Nuneaton

# Why?

The sun rises, a cockerel crows
For what today will bring, no one knows.
In a far-off land a war begins
Blood will be shed until someone wins.

Boys are recruited, the troops are called,
What's happened to this once peaceful world?
The guns are loaded, the bags are packed,
They set off on a never-ending track.

They shoot people they don't even know,
They're feeling sad, their spirits are low.
Their friend is killed, could it get any worse?
Forever this war they will curse.

The shooting should stop, the wars must end,
The other countries should be our friends.
Many are injured and many die,
It does not end, I ask you why?

**Elise Hiley (13)**
Higham Lane School, Nuneaton

# Pollution

Pollution, pollution everywhere,
Pollution, pollution in the air.
There are plenty of different poisonous fumes
Like evil witches watching us on their brooms.
Pollution, pollution everywhere,
Pollution, pollution in the air.
The wheels on the cars go round and round
The price of petrol is well over a pound.
Pollution, pollution everywhere,
Pollution, pollution in the air.

**Daniel Goodyer (11)**
Higham Lane School, Nuneaton

# Save The Planet

Empty cans and broken bottles,
The Earth is damaged by degrees.
Cars and aircraft foul the air,
Pure air dying, endlessly.

Forests burning - wasteful death,
The Earth is damaged by degrees.
Fire and smoke pollute the heavens,
Pure air dying, endlessly.

Save our future, save the Earth,
Save our planet, by degrees.
Save the cans, the paper, bottles,
Save the air and turn it free.

**Lauren Grant (12)**
Higham Lane School, Nuneaton

# Poor Fat Sammy

I see him on the way to school
Dragging his feet along.
My heavy heart is pounding
As they start to sing the song.

'Fat Sammy, fat Sammy
Runs home crying to his mammy.
Eats ten burgers with lots of chips
Then some crisps and fatty dips.'

Poor fat Sammy
I want to be his friend
But if the other kids saw me
My life would surely end.

**Gemma Miller (12)**
Higham Lane School, Nuneaton

# A Place Not To Be

Guns, guns, guns,
The sound of bullets being shot
Ringing in your ears.
Travelling at light speed,
Pierces your heart in an instant.

Corpses, corpses, corpses
Strewn over the floor.
A stench so bad
Not even Satan
Himself could survive it.

Fire, fire, fire,
One click of a finger
And you're burnt alive.
The pain
Unimaginable.

Bombs, bombs, bombs
Send you flying
Everywhere.
Rocks, bricks,
People, bodies.

Snipers, snipers, snipers,
You're being watched.
One shot and you're dead.
Always wary,
Careful.

Concentration camps, concentration camps, concentration camps,
You'll die.
The lack of gas
All the life
Being literally smoked out of you.

War, war, war,
The one place not to go.

**Sanjay Patel (12)**
Higham Lane School, Nuneaton

# We're All Killers

Fresh smelling grass
Lush emerald-green.
Rainbow-coloured flowers
Smell sweet and sugary.
Dense rainforests
Smell hot and damp.
Rivers sparkle in the sun
Smelling cool and calm.

We are murdering
We are destroying
Our beautiful Earth
Dying at our hands.

Grass shrivels down
Smelling dead and dry
Flowers fade to grey
Smelling putrid.
Rainforests fall with thuds
Smells of burnt wood.
Rivers fill with filth
And smell of acid.

**Paige Ellis (11)**
Higham Lane School, Nuneaton

# Saving The World

The razor beams rise again, the monster within starts its play
Letting fumes come and destroy the outside world.
Everything shrivels up and dies as the monster rolls past.
The churning sound flees all, the choking gas invading our lives.
We enhance the toxic waste and throw it back at the outer world.
The monstrous beast enjoys its work, no holds barred.
When the beast has finished, it rests for another day's work.

**Reece Cooper (11)**
Higham Lane School, Nuneaton

# The Human Race

The human race, where did they go wrong?
On their own once again
Suffering quietly in extreme pain
To keep some in extreme wealth,
Most end up with really poor health.
We do not just destroy ourselves
We put creatures' heads high upon our shelves.
From the world, the energy we drain
We do not make any further gain.
So many things we need to protect
Others are deciding to neglect.
This is the world as we know it
Described by a simple ten-year-old poet
We need to find help, I wonder who.
I know someone, how about you?

**Connah Forster (11)**
Higham Lane School, Nuneaton

# Making The World A Better Place

Save energy to make the world less polluted,
Save food to help the homeless become less starved and hungry,
Save waste and reuse it to help the world recycle
And remember the three Rs.
Help our devastated world,
Help our polluted sky,
Help our weather,
Please just help the world.
Why is it burning hot?
Why is it freezing cold?
Nobody understands why the world's climate is changing
Please save our wonderful world.

**Cameron Fox (11)**
Higham Lane School, Nuneaton

# Think And Save Our World

We only have one life to live so live it to the max
Though if you continue polluting and wasting, you won't be living right now.
When you find some rubbish on the floor, think of the consequences or find a bin and put it in.
No regrets, no hard feelings, that's step one done.
You're on the verge to kill again, the animals are next
You don't realise what good they do, they save our planet but how do you?
Before you damage Earth completely, remember the phrase: 'Stop, look, listen!'
Recycle, recycle, it's as easy as pie but some people over Africa don't even get pie.
God will work with you and hold you together, tell everyone you know. Why oh why? Just think . . .

**Jade Aston (11)**
Higham Lane School, Nuneaton


# Always Look On The Bright Side Of Life

The grass is green and lush over the fence
Why the rest of us have to pay pence.
The homeless, the happy, the ashamed, the neglected
All share the world whether rich or protected.
What's happened to the youth of today
Racism and bullying, why can't they play?
We must remember what we can do,
As there's a bright side you must recognise too.

**Megan Wainwright (11)**
Higham Lane School, Nuneaton

# Bleaching The Great Barrier Reef

The transparent blanket covers a plethora
Of mystical things in the Great Barrier Reef
It covers 1% of the Earth's surface
We're hunting the hunters
We're killing and destroying this planet.

Open up your eyes to the suffering
Stop hunting
Stop polluting the undersea exquisite rainforest
The coral is to an extreme
The clearness of the water is amazing to the human eye
*Stop now!*

**Matthew Wainwright (11)**
Higham Lane School, Nuneaton

# Making The World A Better Place

Save energy to make the world greener
Recycle your unwanted uses
To keep the planet a better place.

Keep animals away from harm
Protect the animals we have
To keep the planet a cleaner place.

Make houses for the homeless
And keep them out of danger
To keep the environment a better place.

Stop pollution altogether
To end the suffer, the sadness and the war
To keep the planet a safer place.

**Amber Burdett (12)**
Higham Lane School, Nuneaton

# Untitled

Many people take for granted
The things we get each day
Unfortunately it's not the case
In some places far away.

Children suffer every day
With AIDS and other illness
We expect presents and gifts
They are thankful for parents.

So how can we make a difference
To all these homeless children
Dropping resources does help
But doesn't get the job done.

So let's take into consideration
People less fortunate
While we're moaning and crying
About something we haven't got.

**Samuel Lissaman (11)**
Higham Lane School, Nuneaton

# Time Is Running Out

The end of the world is near
Pollution is the thing to fear
Endangered animals are dying
Global warming is causing the frying
The ozone layer is being thinned
More suncream is needed or we'll be singed
The eco-systems are collapsing quickly
The polar ice caps are melting more swiftly
Unless we pull our fingers out
There will be nothing left to talk about.

**Ben Smith (11)**
Higham Lane School, Nuneaton

# Why?

Why oh why do we punish the land?
Why oh why do we ravish its beauty?
Can't we look after our splendour and protect our Earth?

Why oh why do we pollute the water?
Why oh why do we waste food?
Why don't we help kids in Africa and open our eyes to the suffering?

Why oh why do we litter?
Why oh why do we kill the animals?
Why don't we recycle and protect our Earth's future?

Why oh why do we chop down rainforests?
Why oh why do we waste our resources?
Can't we reprocess our paper and not clutter up the landfills?

Why oh why do we gas the Earth in petrol?
Why oh why do we smog the ozone with diesel?
Can't we walk to school and use public transport?

Why oh why don't we adopt an endangered animal?
Why oh why don't we sponsor a rainforest?
Why pollute?
Why kill our children's future?
Why?

**Nate James (11)**
Higham Lane School, Nuneaton

# Eco-World

Why pollute our world with cars, trains and trucks,
Why not use solar or wind power?
Why do animals have to suffer?
Racism and war are destroying our world; if we all get together we can fight
against problems
Animal cruelty, racism against others, not wasting food is another
Foie gras is cruel.
Would you like to be the one to suffer?

**Sarah Brown (11)**
Higham Lane School, Nuneaton

# The Plane

It's seen its days of stormy skies
The whip of rain upon its sides
But enjoyment is always lost
From pollution and fuel cost
Soon enough its days would end
It would be anchored to the ground
But pollution that was prevented
Is the one thing that leaves it rejuvenated
The world is now a better place
And altogether it has been abandoned
It still inspires a dream or two
Of soaring in the skies
Wind blowing on your sides
And skies clear and blue.

**Joseph Smith (12)**
Higham Lane School, Nuneaton

# War

Swords, guns and knives,
These weapons can take away your lives
Judging people by their colour, not knowing that they were like each other
A terrible thing, war.
Screaming and shouting, horrible sounds
People lying dead on the ground.
A terrible thing, war.

**Zoha Akram (10)**
Leicester High School for Girls, Leicester

92

# Our Environment

G is for the fresh green grass we lie down on
R is for recycling paper, glass and aluminium
A is for air which we pollute from factories and cars
P is for pollination, for the reproduction of seeds and plants
P is for planet Earth which might be destroyed if we don't care for it
L is for the leaves that fall off trees
E is for the electricity we waste.

**Zarah Kassam (10)**
Leicester High School for Girls, Leicester

# Improving The World

Improving the environment is our main focus now
We're trying to make it green and clean, but how?
First thing, switch off the lights and turn off that tap
After that I suggest compost too
Then buy an electric car, especially for you
Now the world is saved.

**Julia Banerjee (10)**
Leicester High School for Girls, Leicester

# Global Warming Has Arrived

Global warming has arrived
The furry animals are quickly dying
We need to help them
The polar bear is thirsty
The fishes cannot swim
There is no water
We need to help them
The ice is plunging down
Their homes are being destroyed
We could have helped them
Now it's too late
The animals are extinct
The water has evaporated
The ice has melted
We could have helped them.

**Misbah Kassam (10)**
Leicester High School for Girls, Leicester

# Stop!

Right, it's time to change the world
And so you lazy lot get up on your feet
Start saying sorry to the people you've hurt
Stop saying stuff about people's skin colour
We're all the same, shame, shame, shame.
It's not very nice, would you like it too?
No, no, no, I don't think so
And if you're not prepared to change the world
Then you're gonna face the consequences too.

**Priya Patel (10)**
Leicester High School for Girls, Leicester

# Global Warming

P ollution and poverty
L et's all help
A nimals are in danger
N obody is caring
E veryone come on and start recycling
T rees are being cut down

Help save our planet.

**Jemay Patel (10)**
Leicester High School for Girls, Leicester

# Global Warming

Global warming has arrived
The icebergs are melting
The icebergs are melting
How can we stop it?
How can we stop it?
The sea level's rising
The sea level's rising
And it's too much to control.

**Maariyah Sabat (10)**
Leicester High School for Girls, Leicester

# The Polar Bear Poem

Seals, polar bears, our Arctic friends
We're destroying their home.
They need to roam and to be free
They have a life the same as ours
Except they don't cause global warming from their cars
So save these cute furry friends or in thirty years or so
Their population will be a complete meltdown.

**Olivia Scuplak (10)**
Leicester High School for Girls, Leicester

# Poverty

P eople round the world are poor
O nly have a penny
V irtually nothing to eat or drink
E ver living on what they have
R aise money
T ry not to waste
Y ou can give them a home and get a smile on their face.

**Urvi Sedani (10)**
Leicester High School for Girls, Leicester

# Environmental Poem

E xhausts taking over the planet
A ppalling conditions
R acism is getting worse
T oasting antics
H omeless people.

**Katherine Toome (10)**
Leicester High School for Girls, Leicester

# Things We Can Change

Pollution and poverty is bad
So it makes me sad
Climate change and war
Is not what we're born for
Animals are becoming extinct
So their lives are on the brink
Let's stop it together
Forever and ever and ever.

**Morgan Williams (10)**
Leicester High School for Girls, Leicester

# Recycling Is Good

When we have a lot of waste
Some of us forget to recycle
Recycle paper, plastic and glass
To help our Earth survive we must
Use the three Rs whenever we can,
Reduce, reuse and recycle.
Plastic bottles, mobile phones, batteries and Coke cans.
Recycling saves a lot of energy for us to watch TV and to play on computers.
There is so much waste just piled on the planet
Please don't add to it, put a stop to it.
Most people drive to work or to school
But how do you travel when you go to places?
Every morning there is a lot of traffic
If most of us are environmentally-friendly then there won't be as much
We wouldn't have to put up with waiting or being late,
We would be happy rather than miserable,
Buses are bad enough to the planet
So don't make it worse by adding more cars.
Everyone, take public transport, ride your bicycle or walk to where you have to
go
But just remember, save our planet.

**Seetal Assi (10)**
Leicester High School for Girls, Leicester

# Go Green Day

Save the planet and everything in it
Recycle your rubbish
Make the world glitter
Take public transport
Save the planet and everything in it.

**Shriya Amin (10)**
Leicester High School for Girls, Leicester

# Help The World Go Green

The ice caps are melting, help!
The air is polluted, help!
The fumes that come from cars
Could reach right up to the stars.
If we keep on hurting the world
Who knows what will occur?

Animals are becoming extinct
The trees cut down to sticks.
Who knows what will happen
If we don't stop this mayhem?
Recycle, *yes!*
Cut down on miles on cars? *Yes!*
Donate? Yes, yes, *yes!*
All these are tips to help the world go green.

**Anna Galeva (10)**
Leicester High School for Girls, Leicester

# Pollution

Hundreds and hundreds of years ago
This world was in good condition
Then people's cars had a lot of emissions
This made the world in really bad condition.

This world needs your help!
Don't wait for it to get even worse
The Amazon is going to burst
This whole world is cursed.

Pollution, pollution please go away
You're polluting all the air away.
Please go far, far away
Hoping to never see you again.

**Ayesha Aziz (10)**
Leicester High School for Girls, Leicester

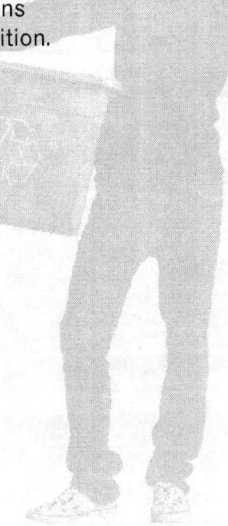

# Environmental Poem

Recycling
Is very good.
It saves the water
And the woods. It keeps
The smoke out of the sky and
Out of your lungs and your eyes.
Recycling is terrific thing. What's
Trash to one is another's bling. When
You reuse stuff; you're a hero and lighten
The landfill load to zero. There's lots of stuff
You can recycle. Make a wheelbarrow from an
Old bicycle. Old milk cartons soon become, a park
Bench you can sit upon. Old Levis become new pencils
And used soap bottles parts of fences. They grind up glass
And melt it down, then shape it again for the next go round. Wood
And glass and cardboard boxes, plastic, paper, aluminium, toxins.
Refrigerators, TVs, used car parts, toys and clothes and even art. If
We all recycle a bunch, things will be better, I have a hunch.
And if we don't, oh me, oh my, I think
We can
Kiss our
Earth
Goodbye.

Litter should not be done!
Do you think the Earth thinks it's fun?
Don't leave litter on the ground.
Come on, pick it up and don't just stand around!
Come now; pick it up with a garbage bag.
You're going to make animals gag.
No more games, no more fun.
Even the sun doesn't like it to be done!
The Earth feels blue, how about you?
This is bad not very glad.
This will make pollution bad!

Stop waste
Stop pollution
And reduce wastage
Save nature and protect Mother Earth.

**Ashni Badiani (10)**
Leicester High School for Girls, Leicester

# Our Earth

The Earth is our home
In it we live
Whether it's England or Rome
To it we should give.

No waste, no litter,
Energy we save.
Don't be so bitter
As God's gift He gave.

Animals and extinction
Rainforest pollution.
Give up your temptation
To solve the solution.

So believe what you hear
Pollution is increasing.
Destruction is near
To the world we are ending.

This we can tackle
Reduce, reuse, recycle.

**Ammaarah Omar (10)**
Leicester High School for Girls, Leicester

# Green

Homelessness, war, litter and terrorism
Poverty, climate change and pollutions
Recycling, charity, kindness, anti-racism,
Some of the problems and some of the solutions.

**Priya Bhalla (10)**
Leicester High School for Girls, Leicester

# The Rainforest

I am standing in the blazing hot sun
Shining away at my roaring hot branches
As hot as a cooker.
My bark is slowly disintegrating away,
I can hear, I can hear the sound of a chainsaw
Coming closer and closer, louder and louder.
How much longer will I last,
A few minutes, a few seconds?
The sounds surrounding me
On the left, on the right.
All of my friends dying away,
The cruel humans cutting us down.
Do they really want to kill us?
What are you going to do?

**Alice Marlow (11)**
Leicester High School for Girls, Leicester

# Stop In The Name Of The Earth

Stop in the name of the Earth
We need to stop the mess we're in.
We need to throw all the rubbish in the bin,
We need to stop pollution so we can carry evolution.
We need to go green, we need to go clean.
We need to see the colours around the Earth
This is the place of our rightful birth.
We need to recycle to make the world clean
And this makes the grass and trees more green.
We must sort this matter to make this world much better.

**Rubean Kaur Kundi (10)**
Leicester High School for Girls, Leicester

# Recycling Race

R ecycle all you can
E ven recycle your cans
C annot face to lose
Y ou're every little help
C an it make this world a better place
L et's find out and see
I f we win the recycling race of course
N ight and day we have to recycle
G etting closer to the end of the recycling race

R ecycling race about to end
A ll recycling bins are outside to compare
C an you see who's won?
E veryone!

**Nima Patel (11)**
Leicester High School for Girls, Leicester

# Extinction

Everyone is coming to see me
As I'm the only one left
I'm the only guinea pig left
The whole world is coming.
I hid myself away from them
Under a pile of mud and grass
I'm the only guinea pig left
The whole world is coming.
I hid for days and days
And soon I was dead
There are none of us left
There are no guinea pigs left!

**Anjani Jogia (11)**
Leicester High School for Girls, Leicester

# Come On You Lot, Do Your Bit!

Come on you lazy ones
Get up, onto your feet and make the world a better place
What could you do?
Pick up the litter so your pets or wild animals don't eat it
Because that might cause them to have a nasty tummy ache.
Or even encourage your older brothers and sisters,
Mum and dad or even your grandma or grandpa
To walk to the corner shop down the road instead of taking the car.
You could even try cycling to school and that would stop pollution.
Just try and do one tiny thing a day.

**Devina Pathak (10)**
Leicester High School for Girls, Leicester


# Pollution

No one knows what to do anymore
I look at the people left, I should have known
People in their cars driving on and on.

I look at the birds up in the sky
Oil, petrol, pollution, they're struggling to fly!
No one cares anymore, if only they'd thought before
We wouldn't be in this mess, maybe an idea!
They're not bothered anymore
In the distance I can see fumes, they're still working, they don't care
They just want the money.
No one cares anymore, no one's bothered
People, crying and I just want to help.

**Shreya Patel (11)**
Leicester High School for Girls, Leicester

# Environment Poem

Danger, danger upon us
Icebergs melting
Ozone layer dying
Hurricanes rushing.

Tidal waves drowning people
Mankind killing Mother Nature
Earthquakes causing disaster
Warning, danger, danger upon us.

**Annika Amin (11)**
Leicester High School for Girls, Leicester

# Spare Change

'Spare change Sir? Spare change?'
A little child, so small, so fragile,
No money, no clothes, no home.

They all come, they all crowd.
'Spare change Sir? Spare change?'
No smiles, no laughs, just frowns.

I turn, I walk, my tears flowing fast
My ears ringing with their voices.
'Spare change Sir? Spare change?'

Their skeletal faces skinny, frail, pale
And dead, sunken eyes.
The image burned in my mind.

A young girl a water bucket in hand
Water. Is it? It can't be.
So dirty, so murky, it can't be!

A baby in rags on his own, alone.
Crawling towards me, face pleading weakly.
A home, please give me a home.

This village, these children,
Drained of all home.
Who is it? The culprit, poverty.

**Tia Ralhan (11)**
Leicester High School for Girls, Leicester

# People Don't Care

Empty beer bottles floating in the sea
Poor dolphins dying, trapped in a net full of fish
People don't care; they think they make a lovely dish.
Whales caught in China and sold to eat
Little penguins in the Arctic dying on their feet.

**Priyanka Mistry (11)**
Leicester High School for Girls, Leicester

# Cars Polluting

Cars get us from A to B
So how bad can they really be?

Fossil fuels from underground
Are burned in cars which are all around.

The gases that all cars emit
Are full of pollutants, you've got to admit.

Cars get us from A to B
So how bad can they really be?

The tyres never rot down
So they are dumped all around.

Cars get us from A to B
So how bad can they really be?

When cars get past their useful days
They are dumped in scrapyards to endlessly laze.

Recycling them would not be cheap
So we leave the cars to rust in a heap.

Cars get us from A to B
This is how bad they can really be.

**Libby Dooher (12)**
Leicester High School for Girls, Leicester

# Poverty

P oor people deserving pity
O ld and frail
V arious problems, various ages
E ver needing
R elief, providing money for the poor
T hings lacking
Y ou people out there, help!

**Gurpreet Kandola (11)**
Leicester High School for Girls, Leicester

# The Last Tree In The Rainforest

Slowly, stiffly, I shake my head
And let my branches droop with a sigh.
For I'm the last tree in the rainforest
And I am soon to die.

I've watched my fellows crash to the ground
Massacred then taken away.
The hunters left the woods, laughing
They'd done with killing for today.
'We'll regroup,' was what everyone said
But the cracks began to show.
More were killed, few were left.
Who would be next to go?

They're coming now, I'm sure I hear them
The whole forest shakes when they are near.
My nerves start to crumble, my heart to pound
And I find my branches shaking in fear.
This time there is no pondering
For there is no one left but me.
This is the end of my era
And I think it's quite sad to see.

Felled then suffocated under a tarpaulin
I hadn't even the breath to cry.
I was the last tree in the rainforest
Before I had to die.

**Rebecca Dennis (12)**
Leicester High School for Girls, Leicester

# Where Have The Trees Gone?

I am woken by the morning breeze
Blowing through the evergreen trees.
But of course for me now, it's all stopped
Those trees are gone, cut, chopped.

I wonder where those trees went
But I know now, I found out last night.
I heard roaring and looked outside,
I saw a man; he held a chainsaw and I know what for.
I hid and cried, I cried making the pillow soggy
I cried like a river flowing into the sea
And I thought, *that's where the trees are going. But why?*

**Aaliyah Esat (11)**
Leicester High School for Girls, Leicester

# Litter

Litter, litter on the ground,
Pick it up and don't you frown.
Don't try and drop your litter,
It will make your life so bitter.

Litter, litter here and there,
Litter, litter everywhere.
You should have a world that's clean,
So pick it up and don't be mean.

Litter, litter dropped on the floor,
Litter is killing animals, we don't want more.
Litter is a deadly sight,
Put it in the bin, we'll make the world right.

**Pooja Mistry (11)**
Leicester High School for Girls, Leicester

# Climate Change

C hoking smoke in the cities
L itter dropped on the streets, people don't seem to care.
I ntensive building on the flood plains
M any countries living in poverty.
A nimals are being hunted to extinction, dying painful deaths.
T oo many cars on the road, polluting the world as they go.
E ducating children of the world as they are adults of tomorrow.

C ontainers transporting recycling to poorer countries
H abitats of animals and tribes being destroyed
A ir pollution caused by too many planes and cheap flights
N uclear power stations being built, is this the way we should go?
G reenhouse gases filling the air
E ncourage people to recycle, reuse and react, before it's too late.

**Clarissa Wells (11)**
Leicester High School for Girls, Leicester

# Loneliness

Where am I?
In a world with no food, love or care.
Where am I?
Living in a cardboard box.
Where am I?
In a world where all I can hear are buses, cars, trains and lorries.
Where am I?
In a world with no warmth, love or care.
I know where I am . . . I'm in loneliness.

**Nimika Patel (11)**
Leicester High School for Girls, Leicester

# The Animals Are Gone

The old days . . .
The polar bears trek across the icy padded snow,
The orang-utans sit above a tree eating the juicy fresh food,
A beautiful glorious world we live in filled with life.

Now . . .
The polar bears stranded on one block of ice, the only one in miles,
The orang-utans lie on the rainforest floor, no trees to sit on or eat,
The evil men have chopped them all down.
An ugly world we live in filled with dying if you don't help.
Where are the polar bears?
Where are the orang-utans?
We live in a world of death!
Save our environment and all that is in it, reduce, reuse, recycle!

**Alicia Mead (12)**
Leicester High School for Girls, Leicester

# Without A Home

Homeless, nowhere to live, don't have enough money.
All the people I see, their life is as sweet as honey.
Lying on the street with nothing to eat.
Shabby clothes, starvation, that's my life.
No one cares about me, my heart's empty.
Running out of energy, the power has all gone
Gently fainting, gently dying
Dead at dawn.

**Sara Saquib (11)**
Leicester High School for Girls, Leicester

# What Has Happened To The World?

What has happened to the world we live in?
It has been cut down, polluted and left to die.
What has happened to the inhabitants who live here?
We do not appreciate the wonders of the world.
We do not care, we do not care.

What has happened to the world we live in?
Nuclear explosions, wars and global warming.
What has happened to the inhabitants who live here?
We have left whole species without their habitats
We have left rivers to run dry but the glaciers are melting.
We do not care.

What has happened to the world we live in?
We have made bombs, military hardware and weapons out of its natural
resources.
What has happened to the inhabitants who live here?
We raid the Pyramids and destroy ancient palaces.
We take no heed of the world's warnings, of global warming and overflowing seas
We do not care.

What has happened to the world we live in?
Soon fish and plankton will be dying on our riverbanks
Whole continents will be swallowed.
What has happened to the inhabitants who live here?
We have let greed and money take us over
We do not care.

**Olivia Choudhury (12)**
Leicester High School for Girls, Leicester

# World Clean? Be Green!

Clear the world, be good boys and girls,
Turn off the lights or you'll see bad sights.
Save energy and oil, it's too precious to spoil.
Recycle boxes in bins, everything including tins.
You need to be green to keep the world clean.

A hundred years on the world will be gone,
No money, not funny, no food to fill our tummy.
No heating, no eating, all waste will be reeking.
No soil, no oil because no one was loyal.
No glass, no brass, people dying fast.
No cans, no pans, everywhere a sham.
No sun, no fun, rubbish weighing tonnes.
No silver, no gold, no story to be told.
You need to be green to keep the world clean.

**Lilly Atkinson (13)**
Leicester High School for Girls, Leicester

# The Touch Of War

When I think of war
I see children crying, women weeping, soldiers dying on the blood-stained grass.
When I think of war
I hear the distant guns shooting innocent men.
When I think of war
I smell the houses burn, consumed in vicious flames.
When I think of war
I taste disgusting, rationed porridge grinding in my mouth.
When I think of war
I feel goosebumps crawling up my skin.
When I think of war
I hope for a solution and a change in the world.

**Anna Tulchinskaya (12)**
Leicester High School for Girls, Leicester

# No Future

I'm a happy polar bear
I have thousands of fish to eat
And good friends around me
Lots of space to roam around
That's how it used to be but now . . .

I'm a lonely polar bear
My food is very scarce with barely any left
There are few polar bears around
I feel I'm the only one here
I don't think I have a future.

I'm a lonely polar bear
I live on an isolated frozen iceberg
In the middle of the sea, nowhere to go, silence
I don't think I have a future.

I'm a lonely polar bear
Our population is dropping
Our food and habitat is being demolished
Our hope is very little
I don't have a future.

**Hannah Pepler (12)**
Leicester High School for Girls, Leicester

# Reduce! Reuse! Recycle!

One for the money
And two for the waste
You can see a green box
So don't put it in the bin
Reduce! Reuse! Recycle!
Three for the environment
And four for the world
You can see a green box
So don't put it in the bin
Reduce! Reuse! Recycle!
Two sides of a paper, one not being used
Being chucked in the bin
But not the green box
Green boxes everywhere around school
We need them to be used as tools
Use these boxes to recycle
The paper will go in
So the cycle begins
This will be good for me and the world
And now it's good for you too
So reduce, reuse, recycle!

**Radika Shikotra (12)**
Leicester High School for Girls, Leicester

# The World

The world is alive
But we can't survive
And soon it will come to an end.

What shall we do?
Give us a clue
How can we help the world?

We ask Gordon Brown
But all he does is frown.
Will pollution always be around?

Racism is really strong
But we know it's wrong.
Let's stop it from going on.

Now if it were done
We could all have fun
And carry on with our lives.

**Eleanor Turner (12)**
Leicester High School for Girls, Leicester

# Stranded

Poor little polar bear
Stranded on a block of ice
Poor little polar bear
All he wanted was something delicious and nice.

Poor little orang-utan
Left sitting on the ground.
No mother, no father, no trees to play on,
Nowhere to sleep.

Poor little elephant
For there is nothing left around him.
Poor little elephant
Surrounded by bare open landscape.

Global warming
The animals have no say, *we do!*
The simplest things can help
So come on and do your bit for the world
And make it a better place.

**Eshaa Sidi (12)**
Leicester High School for Girls, Leicester

# Brothers Of War

In the dark mass of the night's sky lies the cold lonely moon.
She glares down at me with envy in her eyes.
How she must wish to live on my planet,
To be a human, to be free, with more than just stars for company.

I can see her now in the blackened sky
As the wind howls in my ears and rustles in the tall grass.
I can hear the heavy clink of boots as I walk forwards,
I hear the frost crunch beneath my feet.

I feel alone yet my friends are right beside me.
We march together in a line, as though we are ghosts
But the men beside me are the closest thing I have,
They are my brothers, my brothers of war.

A gun sounds, our enemies have reached us.
More guns are fired and men begin to fall,
Their cries echoing in the still silent night.

Then there is a noise louder than any other
And flames flicker in and out of view.
My heart stops beating and I fall down dead
With my wounded friends lying beside me.

The last thing I see is the dark night's sky
And the lonely moon with her lonely eyes.

Now I realise that the moon is not envious
For why would she want to live in a world of greed and jealousy?

Why must we fight and why can we not live in peace?
When will humans live in harmony and when will wars cease?

**Ruby Ablett (12)**
Leicester High School for Girls, Leicester

# What Is Going On In Our Environment?

I've written this poem to tell you what is going on in our environment.
We have to make sure that we don't leave our world in abandonment.
I want to tell you about some issues that are green
So that we can help to keep our world tidy and clean.
We are looking for ways to reduce our carbon footprint
So we have to come up with a sensible blueprint.
We shouldn't need permissions
To reduce our car emissions.
We need to deal with all the pollutions
By coming up with sensible solutions.
People are more bothered about using their cellphone
Than helping to stop reducing the layer of ozone.
We are too busy cutting down the rainforests
Than helping people in the world who are the poorest.

Everywhere there is poverty
And we need to have more charity.
On the news we hear about new wars
With deaths read out like football scores.
People seem to be driven by capitalism
Rather than dealing with issues like racism.
We can save the world of many quids
By all becoming caring, active eco-kids!

**Anjali Bhalla (12)**
Leicester High School for Girls, Leicester

# Destroyed Rainforests

The rainforest has colour,
Colours that are bold and bright.
All the animals wide awake
Apart from those who wake at night.
The rainforest is peaceful
So peaceful with only birds chirping.
But, what is that I hear?
It's the tribes drumming.
The rainforest is suddenly noisy,
What has happened?
It is now dull and bleak
And the animals endangered
The rainforest trees are destroyed
It is cold, miserable and wet.
Lots of people living here
But it's not over yet.

**Anisha Patel (12)**
Leicester High School for Girls, Leicester


# Beautiful Blue

I swam out into the sea on a gorgeous day
And gorgeous was the sea
It was the bluest blue and crystal clear
'Twas just me and the beautiful sea.
I waded; I swam out into the blue, the beautiful blue
As far as the eye could see
And then I turned round to see the view that was meant for only me.
I saw the blue with the algae like glue and the plastic bottles too.
Polystyrene foam reminded me of home
Along with the sad garden gnome.
The dead seagull with a fishing net round its wings,
Surrounded by dead fish, the poor little things
This all comes from pollution, make it stop
It was all made by you, so think before you drop.

**Elizabeth Charles (12)**
Leicester High School for Girls, Leicester

# No More War

Another news flash,
People have no other choice but to dash.
War has started,
Countries and people have parted.

Tears and sorrow spreads around,
Dead innocent children lie on the ground.
Those unlucky who have been hit,
Are forgotten, the government not doing their bit.

Villages lit alight with fire,
Jet harriers permanently on hire.
Infrastructure severely damaged,
Lives brutally savaged.

Politicians argue out loud,
Promises are made and valued.
All claiming fame,
To a war undoubtedly lame.

We don't need war,
Leaving people so poor.
So let's all hold hands,
And make a stand.
No more war!

**Ayesha Girach (12)**
Leicester High School for Girls, Leicester

# Litter

L ittering is nasty for our environment
I t is a waste of time and energy
T he right thing to do is to bin it
T ime is of the essence!
E nvironment is important to us
R ecycle, it's not that hard.

**Yasmin Feuozi (12)**
Loughborough High School, Loughborough

# A Ticking Time Bomb

I am dying, *help* me
My timer is ticking
*Tick-tock, tick-tock*

I am dying, *feed* me
My core is weakening
Please save me

I am dying, *release* me
Release me from the burden I carry
I am weary

I am dying, *appreciate* me
My timer *can* be stopped
But I need your help

I am dying, *I am the Earth*
I am the problem
*You can be the solution.*

**Niamh Conway (13)**
Loughborough High School, Loughborough

# War

Dead, dead, all around me,
Dead, dead, is all I see.
Dead, dead, scattered bodies all about,
Dead, dead, I'm glad it's not me.

Blood, blood, smeared on faces,
Blood, blood, is all I see.
Blood, blood, pouring into the ground,
Blood, blood, I'm glad it's not from me.

Why, why, did this happen?
Why, why, should it be?
Why, why, did the Germans push forward?
Why, why? Britain just wants to be free.

**Olivia Kellie (11)**
Loughborough High School, Loughborough

# Recycle For The World

Recycling is like giving to the poor
When you recycle, it makes you feel good.
If you recycle, you help the world even more.
There are green bags, red bags and further yet.
But what is the point, what's recycling for?

If we don't recycle, we could run out of fuel
And then we wouldn't have access to television or anything.
We would all be known as a fool.
One tin can could power your computer for three whole hours
Recycling is one special rule.

There are endless items that can be recycled,
Aluminium to plastic, glass to cardboard.
Trust me, your bin will be filled.
Put all your items into the recycling bin
And then it will be reused, not killed.

**Priya Patel (11)**
Loughborough High School, Loughborough

# Litter

Why did I drop litter on the floor?
Why didn't I come back and pick it up before?
Why did I let the litter man groan
And pick up my litter I left all alone?
Come on kids, let's do our job
And pick up the litter that we all dropped.
We won't let pollution take over us, OK?
We won't let the people in the world complain.
I'm sure if we work as a team,
We'll all start to recycle and become green.

**Krishna Joshi (12)**
Loughborough High School, Loughborough

# How To Make The World A Better Place

Help me to make the world better,
Take a moment to read this letter,
Make sure the public know the damage they've done,
Tell them to change the outcome.
Homeless children starving all the time,
Dirty and cold, wishing to eat at least sometime,
Racism, exclusions, destructions, no future very clear,
Loss, death, extinctions for us all to fear.
Rainforests are being cut down every day,
The world's getting worse, I have to say,
Recycle your paper and we'll get much more,
Than just the small amount of wood left on the floor.
The total of animals on our planet is dropping,
Do not harm them and instead, start protecting,
It's terrible how much pollution and how many wars,
Everybody listen and follow the laws.
Climate change is coming our way,
Let's do our best to have our say,
Don't throw litter on the floor,
There will be more and more.
Recycle your cans, papers and tins,
And throw them away in the right bins.
If you want a brighter future,
Don't pretend it's not your job
And make sure . . . *you go green!*

**Zeinab Rajabally (11)**
Loughborough High School, Loughborough

# The Homeless Girl

She's been sitting there for a while now
Staring at the bleak, grey sky
Because she has no home or family
She suddenly starts to cry.

When old ladies sneer
And children mock
She just sits there
In her tattered grey frock

Nobody cares for her
The world passes by
She's a nuisance, a pest
Who suddenly starts to cry

Are we really so obnoxious?
Have our hearts turned to stone
To leave this vulnerable woman
On the streets, on her own?

So help homeless people like her
Slowly rebuild their life
And save countless people
From heartache and strife.

**Ayesha Kotecha (13)**
Loughborough High School, Loughborough

# Global Warning!

Global warming is a warning!
Recycle now, don't wait till morning.
Here are some tips that you can follow:
Don't leave your grandchild in future sorrow.
Fill your red bags with paper and card,
If you think about it, it's not that hard!
In the green bags it's plastic and tin,
It's pointless just throwing it in the bin!
Waste not, want not,
It's the same with water,
If you don't save now,
People's lives will be shorter!
Showers, not baths,
Turn off taps,
This is easy, much simpler than maths!
All these little things that you can do,
Can help the world and your grandchild too!

**Evie Marshall (12)**
Loughborough High School, Loughborough

# Hunting For Me

Hunted for my fur
Hunted for my horns
Hunted day and night
I hide out of sight

Lucky I'm not dead
One of one hundred left
My habitat's destroyed
*Bang!* The dreaded noise

Helpless, vulnerable
Exhausted, my heart thumping
Scared, sad and angry that
All my friends have gone.

**Jessica Rothberg (11)**
Loughborough High School, Loughborough

# Be Keen To Be Green!

Rainforests are being chopped down,
Animals are just dying out,
Litter is all over the town,
It's a big problem, there's no doubt.

There is pollution everywhere,
So the climate changes rapidly,
There are factories here, factories there,
Puffing out smoke continuously.

Our planet is not fit,
We all need to act *now*,
We must do something to save it,
And that's a fact, but how?

We can start by one of these,
Carry on to recycle,
Plant things, especially trees,
Walk, or even cycle.

**Shushan Li (11)**
Loughborough High School, Loughborough

# Litter

No litter helps
Make the world a better place
It is good
To the human race.

It helps save animals
It helps save us
It won't get caught
In the wheels of a bus.

So don't leave litter
Lying on the ground
Or you will pay
A whole one pound.

**Charlotte Wood (11)**
Loughborough High School, Loughborough

# The City Of Jade

A rumbling sound awakens me and I fly up in the air,
Nothing can harm me here.
I look down in fear as a giant wave runs out over the emerald sea.
As the tide disappears over the horizon, I see the ground,
It is no longer dazzling green, but muddy brown.
My home is gone, destroyed alongside many others.

So when you finish off your dining room with a tropical wood table,
Think of my home, destroyed in creating yours.
And when you sit down to your roast beef,
Think of the land that was used for less than three years before
it was stripped bare,
To be abandoned in order to fatten the cows.
We go hungry.
Think of medicines we could find in our rainforest larder.
So, as you threatened us with death,
Think of your own kind who may die for a cure
That could have been found in the city of jade,
The land of green,
Green that is ever decreasing.

**Hannah Kent (11)**
Loughborough High School, Loughborough

# Act Now

Continued pollution,
World execution!
Carry on,
World gone!

Go green,
Improvement seen!
Work together,
World forever!

**Harriet Cooper (11)**
Loughborough High School, Loughborough

# Keep The Earth Clean!

The world gets upset,
And it needs to reset.
Clean up your act,
This is a fact.
Recycling is so much fun,
It doesn't leave a single crumb.
Boxes, cardboard, paper and mags,
All need to go in single red bags.
Plastic goes in green bags,
But not for your dirty rags.
Get a biscuit from the tin,
When finished, put it in the bin.
Don't drop litter on the floor,
Especially gum and apple core.
Keep the pavement clean,
So people don't know where you've been.
All this is easy to do,
Just make sure you do, do, do!

**Amelia Short (11)**
Loughborough High School, Loughborough

# The Rainforest

A flourish of colour and light, of noise and excitement
I rejoice in the toucan's song
I drink from the cool water
But there is a noise in the distance
A far-off rumbling sound that is not welcome here
Alarm and panic runs through the creatures' hearts
As they scream their warning
Yellow tractors in the distance, trampling over trees
Can I stop them, or will they roll over me, just like the trees?
But whatever I do, I must try.

**Alexandra Abraham (11)**
Loughborough High School, Loughborough

# Go Green

Don't turn your head away,
Save your planet today,
Recycle, go green and keep the world clean.
Recycle, recycle the rubbish we waste,
Don't throw that rubbish away in haste,
Filling the landfill with the rubbish we waste,
Making the Earth a miserable place.

Turn off the lights when you go out,
To stop wasted electricity coming out!
Driving your car little and far,
Is not helping the atmosphere by far!
Punching fumes into the air,
Making me feel like we don't care!

**Evie Crane (11)**
Loughborough High School, Loughborough

# I Am Homeless

I am homeless
I live on the street
With the gutter at my feet
And not a morsel to eat.

I am homeless
People look at me and stare
I tell you it's not fair
At least something warm to wear.

I am homeless
Someday I'll have somewhere to live
Some love of my own to give
But for now I've just hope
As I'm homeless.

**Hannah Clayton (12)**
Loughborough High School, Loughborough

# If I Were A Bear

If I were a bear
And a polar bear too
I would really care
If it was sunny or it snowed.
My food is slowly disappearing
What is my favourite dish?
Believe it or not
It's a big, juicy fish.
The sea is getting higher,
My home's getting smaller,
The ice is about the size of a tractor's tyre
The pollution doesn't help
And neither do you!
But guess what! Here's what to do
*Save the polar bears*
*And*
*Stop global warming!*

**Radhika Tandon (11)**
Loughborough High School, Loughborough

# Reduce, Rehome, Recycle

Litter, litter
How can it be so bitter?
Clogging up our streets
And our lifestyles too.

Pollution, pollution,
We need a solution.
Climate change and
Global warming too.

I'm homeless, I'm homeless,
I'm cold and I'm hungry.
I'm homeless, I'm homeless,
Wild animals beware.

**Nicole Harvey (12)**
Loughborough High School, Loughborough

# Something Must Be Done

Far distant cries of help I hear,
I feel the endless hunger,
I scent a smell of dust and dirt,
And see the death of the younger.

Around this place is nothing,
Nothing worth to see.
Only people who are suffering,
Suffering to be free.

Children not even given a chance,
A chance to have a life.
No education, no occupation,
No more than trouble and strife.

I hear a voice inside my head,
'Something must be done!'
I feel the urge to do something,
I see a battle to be won!

**Charlotte Rowell (11)**
Loughborough High School, Loughborough

# Fighting For Today

Bombs drop from the sky,
Another death, another cry.
Soldiers travel far away,
Fighting for us, for today.

Everybody tries to move on,
But it simply cannot be done.
Too many lives have been lost,
*All this really has to stop!*

**Reeya Chandarana (13)**
Loughborough High School, Loughborough

# How Can We Help?

It is hard to be green,
Because you have to be keen,
Global warming is an issue,
And could shorten our lives too.

Make the world a better place,
For the human race.

Planting trees near your home,
Painting your house a light or dark tone,
Insulate your walls,
And shorten your calls.

Make the world a better place,
For the human race.

Walk, bike, take the bus or car share,
Save energy or the bill could be a scare,
Light the fire or put a jumper on,
Or sit in the sun.

Make the world a better place,
For the human race.

Reduce waste of food,
Reusing bottles you could include,
Recycling plastic or tin
And never bin.

Make the world a better place,
For the human race.

If we all pull together,
Our ideas being clever,
We can bring global warming to a standstill,
And do energy-efficient jobs at your will.

**Isabel Hopwood (11)**
Loughborough High School, Loughborough

# My Love For The Polar Bear

I've always loved the polar bear,
I didn't know he needs my care.
He is so white,
And full of might,
And seemed so safe within his lair.

But climate change is mightier still,
Quiet and deadly, ready to kill.
Just like a man,
Does what he can,
To make a healthy planet ill.

All us children must not let,
The polar bear go just yet.
It's to my taste
To stop this waste,
From car and train and boat and jet.

**Kate Holberry (11)**
Loughborough High School, Loughborough

# Helping Numbers!

1, 2, 3, plant a tree,
4, 5, 6, help a charity,
7, 8, 9, sponsor a lion,
10, 11, 12, put on a jumper,
13, 14, 15, fill up your water bottle,
16, 17, 18, go on a litter hunt,
19, 20, remember every little helps!

**Charlotte Ellison (11)**
Loughborough High School, Loughborough

# No Innocent War

In the mountains, on the beach,
A scream, a cry, a shout, a screech.
It matters not, day or night,
For the sky is ablaze with shots and light.
And what of the innocent who flee from the gun?
Why are they here, why must they run?
A mother and child, a father and son,
Cower together, in the midnight sun.
The tanks and the weapons are all around,
As bodies about them fall to the ground.
But what of the soldiers, who lay down their lives?
They are brave, but with children and wives.
Controllers sit and launch warheads,
Air strikes and bombings leave towns in shreds.
Marching and shooting, it's all they can do,
Past enemy lines with only smoke as a view.
Whether it's the Nazis, Russians or Taliban at war,
In the Somme, Crimea or Gaza, for
We know that there will be death and destruction,
As fighting is such a waste and obstruction.

Whether the berets are green or blue,
We're all still humans through and through.
Stop the fighting, stop the death,
Let the victims take one more breath.
Show them mercy, show them peace,
Let the world's sadness ever cease.

**Rachel Grewcock (12)**
Loughborough High School, Loughborough

# Homeless

I sit on the streets all day,
Wishing I knew what to say.
What a home is like,
But I can't even get a bite!
Sometimes I think,
What it is even like to have a drink.
But for now,
I only allow
To think strong,
I won't be here for long.
How I wish I had a home,
Instead of being all alone!

**Millie Lord (12)**
Loughborough High School, Loughborough

# Recycling Land

Make the world a better place
For us to live in, the human race,
Plastic cans, cardboard and tins,
Remember to put in your recycling bins.
These giant monsters side by side,
Dominate a household's lives.
Paper rustles! Bottles clang!
The music of recycling land.

The latest 'must have' on suburban streets
Are water butts and compost heaps.
Shoppers armed with life-long bags,
Would see the end to the plastic bag.
Littering our countryside, blowing through city streets,
Discarded ghosts of the shoppers' treat,
Make the world a better place,
For us to live in, the human race.

**Frances Christian (12)**
Loughborough High School, Loughborough

# The Rainforest

Green canopies towering magnificently above,
The fresh dewfall gradually sifting over the rainforest
Rainfall hammering like the beat of a drum, bouncing off the foliage.

Twisting vines draped over the trees,
Footfalls racing over the covered floor,
Beautiful melodies echoing from tree to tree.

The scorching sun visible behind an umbrella of jungle-like leaves,
The breathtaking views of perfectly arched rainbows,
The occasional glance of tropical birds, swiftly gliding in all directions.

The silhouette of the still moon,
The stars brilliantly bright,
Peace all around.

The sunrise, a merge of fabulous colours,
The sky, admired by all.
The blissful, striking colours, in the rainforest.

**Lucy Summerton (12)**
Loughborough High School, Loughborough

# The Dustbin Man

Litter, litter, on the floor,
Litter, litter, please no more.

All day I spend,
Going round the bend,
Picking up rubbish, there is no end.

Litter, litter, on the floor,
Litter, litter, please no more.

Some day I hope,
Some day I pray,
That all this litter will go away.

Litter, litter, on the floor,
Litter, litter, please no more.

**Rebecca Moore (12)**
Loughborough High School, Loughborough

# War

The noise is deafening.
It rings in my ears.
People screaming in pain,
Men shooting at things they cannot see,
But we know they're there.

There are men dying at my feet,
I hate it.
I hate the war.
I hate the people who are killing my friends.
That's what keeps me going.
Fighting to kill the people who did this to them.

That morning we sat at the table,
All of us thinking that this could be the last meal
And for some of us it was.

So here we are,
People are still crying out in pain,
People are still dying at my feet.
When will all this stop?
When will the armies put down their guns
And stop the war?

**Abigail Chang (12)**
Loughborough High School, Loughborough

# Save The World

Save the world, it's dying,
The world is crying for help.
The grass is green, the world is clean,
The skies are blue and clear.
There's no rain, the world's not in pain,
The clouds are rolling by.
This is wrong, the grass is gone,
The world is dirty and sick,
The skies are grey, Mother Nature's gone insane.
What have we become?
Are we monsters, destroying the birds,
The streams, the rainforests, the green?
Are we villains, hurting the land, the sea,
The air and the trees?
It's you and me, doing these things,
But we can change,
Counteract the pain.
Is it too late?
We will just have to wait.
Change,
That is all I plead, what the world needs.
That is what will save us -
Change.

**Cassie Ippaso (13)**
Loughborough High School, Loughborough

# Little Things Can Save The World

With all these gases in the air
And a hole being created in the ozone layer,
Nobody knows what to do,
Hoping to make the world cleaner too.
All we can do - me and you
Is help by doing small things. *But how?*
Number one, turn the lights off (if they're not used),
Number two, recycle things like shoes,
Number three, walk, cycle or go on the bus,
It's easy, so why make such a fuss?

There are lots more things to do,
We can do it - me and you,
We can *save the world!*

**Gabrielle Wood (12)**
Loughborough High School, Loughborough

# Too Hot, Too Cold

Wind, rain, sun or snow,
Ice which melts or fog that's thick,
Animals are dying, you say, *so?*
What have these animals done to you?

Polar bears are dying,
Monkeys are falling,
All because of me and you,
Why don't you care? You should do.

No snow at Christmas,
Too hot, too cold,
The world crumbles beneath our feet,
What do we do? *Nothing.*

**Chloe Raikes (12)**
Loughborough High School, Loughborough

**138**

# Recycling

When you're recycling, you're obviously not cycling,
But you're doing something to help save the world instead.
Lose that litter, recycle that waste,
And you'll be helping the world to be a better place.

You know that Coke can lying on the floor,
Don't just walk past it, recycle some more!
Don't be a chicken, recycle lots more,
Don't just leave that newspaper so still on the floor,
When it can be used to make more!

When you're doing the carrots, don't chuck the peelings,
Anyway you might hurt its feelings.
So instead, run down to near the shed
And put it on the compost bed.

You can do that with banana skins too,
So skip down to the compost singing whoopi-doo.
So now you can see by doing this,
You can be a recycling Queen Miss.

**Elizabeth Buswell (12)**
Loughborough High School, Loughborough

# Extinction

Animals die every day
They can't escape the measures hunters will take
Death is a cruel price to pay

Mothers and fathers hide away
Protecting children under a tree, behind a bush
The hunters are here, come what may

Before you buy
Just think, why?
Why should they die?

**Eleanor Jackson (12)**
Loughborough High School, Loughborough

# The Tiger

The tiger is prowling down in the bushes,
She sees prey for her cub and rushes
Forward, only she doesn't know
The safest thing for her to do is go.
She moves slowly and as she creeps,
She sees another tiger that crouches and leaps.
As she follows to help catch the prey,
She realises her cub has gone astray.
She looks around, scared and worried
And sees that the animals around her are hurried
The opposite way and wonders why,
Until she hears a quiet cry.
She runs ahead, towards the sound,
Afraid of the silence all around.
She gets to a clearing and sees on the ground,
A little tiger lying on a mound.
It is her cub, she can tell,
If only hunters could see as well,
That animals have lives to live
And they, like us, can forgive.
If we stopped hunting them,
Then we could live in peace again.

**Rebecca Fox (12)**
Loughborough High School, Loughborough

# Murder Of The Rainforest

It cuts into its lean, muscular flesh
The blood pours out of its body, dripping on the ground
Horrified gasps from its fellows, knowing they are next
All of them dead upon the floor
No survivors
But still machines crunch them up like old twigs
It's murder
Murder of the rainforest.

**Olivia Wright (11)**
Lutterworth High School, Lutterworth

# I Am In A War Zone

One word cries out amongst every other in this place.
I hear a gun fire; I hear the screams of men, women and children.

The once peaceful land has turned into a deadly battleground.
My home is no longer the safe, secure place I once thought it was.
Now it is a haven for killing.

I listen to the world outside; it's silent, then . . . *bang!*
The sound of a tank firing its shot echoes a horrible din
throughout the land.
People are dying out there.
We have lived on war since the dawn of mankind,
But now, war has gone too far.
It's time to end this . . .
*Once and for all!*

**Daniel Smith (12)**
Lutterworth High School, Lutterworth

# Untitled

Watch the world get weaker and weaker
Where it twists and flows it will be no more
No more long green grass to grow
Where the fields give food and the taps give water
Save them and don't hesitate
Where the children play and the parents watch
Soon it will be a deserted watch.

**Lucy Evans (12)**
St Dominic's Priory School, Stone

# What Is It Like Being Homeless?

What is it like being homeless?
I really can't explain
The times I really hate it is when I'm stuck in the rain.
I sleep under the stars at night
Until the morning dawns
The sunlight shines so bright
It hits my eyes like thorns.

What is it like being homeless?
What can I really say?
The policemen all betray me
They say to go away
My clothes are all so smelly
They are starting to fray
And I want some food in my belly
My teeth are starting to decay.

What is it like being homeless?
You really want a home
It would be nice to be comfy and snug
Instead of all alone.
But most of all I want a hug.

What is it like being homeless?
What do you think?
Just think of something like this
That will make your heart sink.

**Olivia Gardiner (13)**
St Dominic's Priory School, Stone

# Recycle, Recycle

Recycle, recycle in the green bin
Recycle, recycle a little green tin
Recycle, recycle as much as you can
Recycle, recycle for the binman.

Animals, animals abused all the time
Animals, animals, scientists do all the crime
Animals, animals, help them now
Animals, animals, they don't know how.

Racism, racism, why is it so?
Racism, racism, let everybody know
Racism, racism, why has it not gone away?
Racism, racism, stamp it out today.

Pollution, pollution, not in the sea
Pollution, pollution, why can't *we?*
Pollution, pollution is killing our planet
Pollution, pollution, *we can stop it!*

**Charlie Urban (13)**
St Dominic's Priory School, Stone

# No More Bear

Polar bear
Extinction scare
Is the air about to tear?
Where there is a bear
There's a scare
Stop the pollution now
Someone tell me how.

**Lauren Bathew (13)**
St Dominic's Priory School, Stone

# Green Is A Magic Colour

Keep it green
Climate change is mean
Let's not have war
Let the animals have more
Let's not litter
And racism is so bitter
Let's stop climate change
Our lives must be rearranged
To recycle
And get on your bicycle
We know the solution
Let's stop pollution.

**Eden Atkinson (14)**
St Dominic's Priory School, Stone

# Earth Is Our Planet

Earth is our planet
Help us to take care
The animals on the ground
And the birds in the air

Rainforests are special
And people are too
Save the planet
Or we'll flush you down the loo.

**Cleo Buckley (12)**
St Dominic's Priory School, Stone

# The Earth

I am the Earth
The grass, the trees
The mud, the sand
And that means to me
The sun, the stars shining down
The Earth is a fine place to live
All litter we find on God's fine ground
As long as life
As dear as me
I am the Earth and that is me.

**Megan Baskeyfield (13)**
St Dominic's Priory School, Stone

# Save The Rainforests

It's our fault.
The beautiful rainforests are now just a few.
If everyone was doing the right thing,
Our world would be more wonderful.
Lots of animals lost their habitat
And caused changes to the global weather patterns.
It's not too late.
Just do what you can!

**Maki Ozawa (12)**
St Dominic's Priory School, Stone

# I Hate The Sound Of Guns

I hate the sound of guns
It does give me quite a shock
I hate the look of bombs
It makes my body lock.

I hate the big green tanks
That go and roll away
To faraway places
And there are some going out today.

I loathe those small fast planes
That make that *zooming* sound
They go this way and that way
I don't want them to be around.

The screams of people make me cry
My mum and dad protect me
When people are running by
But they think I can't see
My silly parents lie.

The people that came here
I really don't like now
They make me have lots of fear
I don't know why they allow . . .

Those big fat bombs that kill us all
The gunshots that hit against my wall.

The planes that fly by
And this day we all did die.

**Lucy Hulme & Olivia Gardiner (13)**
St Dominic's Priory School, Stone

# My Big Green Poem

The wars are unwanted
The wars are unsafe
For the whole world
I have to say
Away with the wars
Away, away
Wars are so harmful
That they have destroyed
The hopes and dreams
Of the people around them.

The wars, the wars
We try to understand
Whether you all fight
For something so grand
If that's not the case
Then away with wars
Away, away
Wars destroy the lives of many
For the men who die every day
To save our lives I have to say
Stop these wars
Stop, stop, stop
And don't let this poem
Ever be forgot!

**Sarah Healings (14)**
St Dominic's Priory School, Stone

# Colours Of Our Planet

Green, green, green
Our rainforest is being chopped down
By a horrible chopping machine
What does it mean?
What does it mean?
This machine,
This machine making us unclean?

Red, red, red
Means stop, stop, stop
If we don't stop you'll face the cop
And you, you, you will pay the price
Of love, love, love and sacrifice!

Pink, pink, pink
Means link, link, link
Of you and he and she
If you don't see what you are doing to me
Then we will no longer be.

Why, why, why
Don't you see, see, see
What the great, He, He
Has made for you and me?
Our great planet is filled with our rubbish
So stop being so sluggish.

Who, who, who
Is responsible?
It's we, we, we
And we can make a difference, you'll see!

**Sally Latham (14)**
St Dominic's Priory School, Stone

# Earth In Danger

You're in the solar system . . . suddenly, you see something,
A blue and green planet sitting there in space spinning silently.
It's beautiful, or is it? Suddenly, you see things,
Rubbish yards filled to the brim,
Landfills reaching up to the pollution-filled skies,
Fumes coming out the back of hundreds of cars,
Scrapyards filled with wrecks.
All you can think of is three words -
*Earth in danger!*

**Ben Beavis (16)**
The Fountains High School, Burton-on-Trent

# Poachers

The world should be free of poachers
They are killing off our animals
If we ban poachers
We should find poachers new jobs
Without poachers animals would be free to roam the world.

**Leon Woodhead (15)**
The Fountains High School, Burton-on-Trent

# Recycling

Pick up your litter,
Make the world a better place,
Throw your rubbish in the bin,
Make it a bright Earth,
Sort your rubbish,
Be more green.

**James Bagnall (15)**
The Fountains High School, Burton-on-Trent

# Pollution

Cars, buses and planes,
They all give off $CO_2$,
So if we walk once in a while,
We can lower $CO_2$ levels.
So if we can, we could save
The environment and the animals.

**Lewis Vincent (15)**
The Fountains High School, Burton-on-Trent

# Young Writers Information

We hope you have enjoyed reading this book - and that you will
continue to enjoy it in the coming years.
If you like reading and writing poetry drop us a line, or give us a call,
and we'll send you a free information pack.
Alternatively if you would like to order further copies of this book
or any of our other titles, then please give us a call or log onto our
website at www.youngwriters.co.uk

Young Writers Information
Remus House
Coltsfoot Drive
Peterborough
PE2 9JX
(01733) 890066